DISCOVERING THE BIBLE

THE BIRTH
of
JESUS

and other New Testament stories

RETOLD BY *Victoria Parker*

✦

CONSULTANT *Janet Dyson*

DISCOVERING THE BIBLE

THE BIRTH of JESUS

and other New Testament stories

RETOLD BY _Victoria Parker_ ❖ CONSULTANT _Janet Dyson_

Contents

Published by Anness Publishing Ltd,
Blaby Road, Wigston, Leicestershire LE18 4SE

Email: info@anness.com

Web: www.annesspublishing.com

Anness Publishing has a new picture agency outlet for images for publishing, promotions or advertising. Please visit our website www.practicalpictures.com for more information.

Publisher: Joanna Lorenz
Managing Editor: Gilly Cameron Cooper
Senior Editor: Lisa Miles
Editorial Reader: Joy Wotton
Produced by Miles Kelly Publishing Limited
Publishing Director: Jim Miles
Editorial Director: Paula Borton
Art Director: Clare Sleven
Project Editor: Neil de Cort
Editorial Assistant: Simon Nevill
Designer: Phil Kay
Information Author: AD Publishing Services
Artwork Commissioning: Suzanne Grant and Lynne French
Picture Research: Kate Miles and Janice Bracken,
Lesley Cartlidge and Libbe Mella
Copy Editing: AD Publishing Services
Indexing: Janet De Saulles
Design Consultant and Cover Design: Sarah Ponder
Education Consultant: Janet Dyson

ETHICAL TRADING POLICY
Because of our ongoing ecological investment programme, you, as our customer, can have the pleasure and reassurance of knowing that a tree is being cultivated on your behalf to naturally replace the materials used to make the book you are holding. For further information about this scheme, go to www.annesspublishing.com/trees

PUBLISHER'S NOTE
Although the advice and information in this book are believed to be accurate and true at the time of going to press, neither the authors nor the publisher can accept any legal responsibility or liability for any errors or omissions that may have been made.

PHOTOGRAPHIC CREDITS
Page 6, (BL), Sonia Halliday Pictures.
Page 12, (BL), Guy Mansfield, Panos Pictures.
Page 26, (BR), Penny Tweedie, Panos Pictures.
Page 46 (BL), The Stock Market.
All other images from the Miles Kelly Archive

The Publishers would like to thank the following artists who have contributed to this book:
Inklink Studio (Virgil Pomfret Agency): Simone Boni, Francesco Petracchi, Lucia Mattioli, Theo Caneschi, Federico Ferniani, Alain Bressan, Loredano Ugolini, Alessandro Rabatti, Lorenzo Pieri, Luigi Critone
Also: Sally Holmes, Rob Sheffield, Vanessa Card, Terry Riley, Peter Sarson, Mark Bergin, Terry Gabbey (AFA), John James (Temple Rogers)
Maps by Martin Sanders

Introduction

ABOUT 2,000 years ago an event happened which was to change the world for ever. Jesus Christ was born. From His birth the modern calendar is dated (although the actual year of Jesus's birth was probably 7BC or 4BC, not the year 0, because a medieval monk made a mistake in his calculations!). Every time we look at a calendar and write down the number of the year, we are reminded of the birth of Christ and the existence of the Christian Church since then.

The story of Jesus's birth and His early years is also very familiar. Even today, when many people are less religious than they used to be, many public Christmas displays will include a Christmas crib with the baby Jesus, Mary, Joseph, the shepherds and the wise men, some angels and a few animals nosing around.

Jesus in the temple
When Jesus was separated from Mary and Joseph in Jerusalem, He went to His father's house, God's temple in Jerusalem, where He amazed the religious elders with His knowledge.

The birth and beginning of Jesus's ministry, or teaching, is one of the most important parts of the Bible story with a clear link to modern times. Yet most of Jesus's early years are completely obscure. Only a few events are recorded in the Gospels. There are so few details that, later, people added to the stories to make them more interesting or exciting, or to make a point. Many of these stories though, have no basis in history.

Even the familiar Christmas story owes more to tradition than to the facts that we are given in the Gospels. The only evidence for Jesus's birth in a stable is the fact that Mary laid him in a manger, which was the normal cot for a newborn child in an ordinary Israelite home. A baby was safer there than on the floor where everyone else slept!

The Christmas story also features the amazing sights of the chorus of angels singing to the shepherds, and a new star appearing in the sky. The events have led

many people to question the truth of these stories. However, the gospel writers include these details to make an important point. The baby Jesus was not an ordinary child. He was the Son of God who came into the world as a human to share human life. His aim was to bring humans and God back together in a relationship of trust and service.

The miracles of Jesus's birth continue as Jesus begins His ministry. The paralysed man is healed outwardly and has his sins forgiven. The madman is made mentally and spiritually healthy again; the centurion's servant is healed, even though many people at the time thought that God did not care for Gentiles (people who were not Jewish). In each case the story enlarges on Jesus's mission: to bring God's forgiveness and to break through the barriers of human pride.

The miracles finish with the great act of stilling the storm. With the voice of the Creator's authority, Jesus bids the waves to be still. "Who is this?" cry the amazed disciples in fear and trembling. The message of the gospel writers is clear: "We believe He is the Son of God." They leave their readers to decide if they are right.

Dead Sea and the wilderness
Before Jesus could begin His ministry in Galilee, He was tempted by the Devil in the wilderness around the Dead Sea. When it was proved He could resist temptation, He began His ministry.

❧ JUDEA AND THE BIRTH OF JESUS ❧

This book covers the birth and early life of Jesus, His baptism by John the Baptist, His temptation by the devil, and the early part of His ministry in Galilee

JUDEA BEFORE JESUS
Luke, Ch. 1.

THE BIRTH OF JESUS
Matthew, Ch. 2; Luke Ch. 2.

JESUS'S EARLY LIFE
Matthew, Ch. 2; Luke Ch. 2.

JESUS BEGINS HIS MINISTRY
Matthew, Ch. 3 & 4; Luke Ch. 4.

THE FIRST MIRACLE
John, Ch. 1 & 2.

JESUS'S MINISTRY IN GALILEE
Matthew, Ch. 8 to 14.
Mark, Ch. 1 to 6; Luke Ch. 3 to 9.
John, Ch. 5.

SERMON ON THE MOUNT
Matthew, Ch. 5 to 11.
Luke, Ch. 6 & 11.

Mary and the baby Jesus
This is a fresco (a painting on a plaster wall) of the Virgin Mary and the baby Jesus. Both are shown with haloes, a sign that they are sacred figures.

Jesus and His Early Life

THE birth of Jesus is one of the most recognized stories from the Bible. Every December millions of people celebrate the birth of the Messiah, God's anointed saviour. In many cases, though, the religious significance of this event, and what it has meant for Christians since, has been forgotten by many people.

The sources for two of the gospels, Matthew and Luke, were probably different. The story of the birth of Jesus in the gospel of Matthew is told very much from Joseph's point of view. Luke's gospel focuses very closely on Mary, mother of Jesus, and on Elizabeth, who was Mary's cousin and the mother of John the Baptist. There is a great deal of detail in Luke's account of the birth of Jesus that relates specifically to Mary. This has led some people to think that Luke's source may have been Mary herself. The writers of Matthew and Luke both agree on the divine part of Jesus's origin, that God Himself was Jesus's father.

There is a huge contrast between the amazing events surrounding Jesus's birth, and the surroundings in which these events took place. The Bible indicates, although does not actually say, that the Son of God was born in a stable surrounded by farm animals. He was laid in a manger, from which animals ate. While there, though, He was visited by the magi, wise men and astrologers from the east, from Babylon or Arabia. The Bible tells us that these men followed a new star to find the baby Jesus. Elsewhere, a great chorus of angels announced the birth of Jesus to the shepherds.

When His parents presented Jesus in the temple, as was the custom, they met Simeon and Anna, two prophets whom God had told of the Messiah's birth, who proclaimed Him the saviour of all the people of the world.

After the events surrounding His birth in Bethlehem, Jesus returned with Mary and Joseph to their home town of Nazareth. This was a small, unimportant town in Galilee, although it was close to several of the main trade routes for the Roman Empire. Jesus spent about the first thirty years of His life there, before He was rejected by the people.

Jesus's mission properly began with His baptism in the River Jordan. He was baptized by his cousin, John the Baptist. At the baptism, God gave a sign to everyone present that Jesus was special. The Holy Spirit descended to Jesus in the form of a white dove, and the voice of God announced that Jesus was His son. These messages from God said two things. God announced to the world that Jesus was the Son of God. He also introduced Jesus to the world as His servant. God was saying that Jesus was the person sent by God to deliver the people of the world from sin and evil.

Before Jesus could begin His ministry, He had to undergo a test. He went into the wilderness around the Jordan valley, and was tempted three times by Satan. The temptations of Jesus explored the idea of what it was to be the Son of God. Jesus's replies to Satan's various challenges strengthened His knowledge of His role and what He would have to do. When Jesus refuses to turn stones into bread to eat, He is putting His trust in God to provide what He needs to survive. Jesus says that we should all forget about obtaining earthly goods. We should trust God to provide us with what we need. Satan also tells Jesus that He should throw Himself off of the roof of the temple. Jesus refused to put God to the test in this way. Jesus shows that He did not need to put God to the test in order to trust Him.

There is also another important point that the writer of the Bible makes in this story. Jesus proved that He had learnt the lessons that God had been trying to teach the Israelites since the time of the Exodus. When Moses was leading the Israelites out of slavery in Egypt, they spent forty years wandering in the desert before they were allowed to enter the Promised Land. They had not learnt to trust God in every way. The answers that Jesus gives to Satan's temptations come from the book of Deuteronomy. They show that He has learnt these lessons, and is ready to begin His ministry.

This map shows the area of Jesus's birth and early life. You can see Nazareth, from where Mary and Joseph set out on the long journey to Bethlehem, where Jesus was born. Jerusalem is where Jesus was presented in the temple, and where Simeon and Anna prophesied His great role.

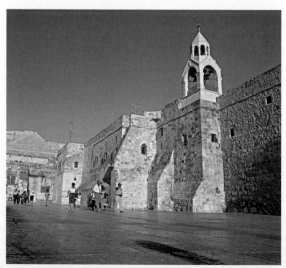

Bethlehem
The Manger Square in Bethlehem is the place of Jesus's birth. The ancestors of King David lived in Bethlehem. Joseph was a descendant of David, born in Bethlehem, so he had to return there for the Roman census, where the Romans counted the population.

MEDITERRANEAN
SEA

•Ptolemais

•Cana

SEA OF
GALILEE

•Hippus

•Sennabris

•Nazareth

•Scythoplis

Caesarea•

•Sebaste

Jordan

•Joppa

•Emmaus

•Jericho

•Jerusalem   •Bethany   •Bethabara

•Bethlehem

DEAD SEA

A Son for Elizabeth

IN the days when King Herod ruled the land of Judea, there was a priest called Zechariah whose wife was Elizabeth. They both tried to live faithfully by the laws of the Jewish religion, but they had one great sadness in their life. They had reached old age without having any children. Still, they always tried to make the most of any happy occasion that came along. One of these occasions was when Zechariah was chosen to be the priest allowed to enter the sacred holy place in the great temple in Jerusalem and burn incense to the Lord. It was a great honour.

The day of the festival arrived and Zechariah dressed in his splendid ceremonial robes, his hands trembling. He could hear his fellow priests singing outside the temple, leading the crowd of worshippers in prayer.

> " *They were both righteous before God.* "

Eventually, Zechariah stood before the incense altar in the holy place itself. With his eyes cast humbly downwards, the aged priest began to burn the sacred incense. And as he spoke aloud the holy passages he had learnt by heart, Zechariah suddenly had the strangest feeling. He was not alone. Someone else was there too, joining him in prayer. Very nervously, Zechariah looked up – and straight away crumpled to the floor with fear. An angel was standing to the right of the altar!

"Don't be afraid, Zechariah," the angel said. "I have come to tell you that your prayers have been answered. You and your wife are going to have a son, whom you must call John. He will bring great happiness not only to you, but also to many other people. The Lord will love him dearly and will send His Holy Spirit to fill your son's heart even before he has been born. Through John, many souls will turn to God. He will prepare the people for the Lord's coming."

The angel Gabriel
A 14th-century stained-glass window shows Gabriel, the angel who announced the news of John's birth. He also told Mary she would have Jesus. Gabriel's name means 'Mighty man of God', and he is one of only two angels named in the Bible (the other is Michael, the warrior angel). He is an archangel who stands in God's presence and takes only special messages into the world.

MOST PEOPLE WOULD FIND IT HARD TO BELIEVE AN ANGEL. THE MESSAGE OF THIS STORY IS THAT GOD EXPECTS HIS PEOPLE TO BELIEVE WHAT HE SAYS, WHICH TODAY IS WRITTEN IN THE BIBLE.

Wailing (Western) Wall
This huge wall in modern Jerusalem is a place of prayer for Jews. It is all that remains of King Herod's temple after the Romans destroyed it. They often leave papers with prayers on them tucked into the gaps between the stones.

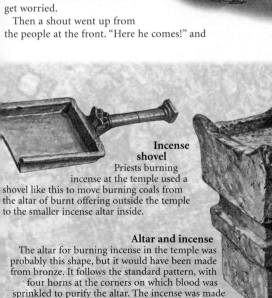

Zechariah was totally stunned. "But... Why... How..?" he stuttered. "We're too old to have children. How can this be true?"

"I am Gabriel," the angel thundered, and Zechariah cowered in terror. In heaven, the angel Gabriel stood at the side of God Himself. "I have been sent by the Lord to bring you this good news," he said. "Because you don't believe what I say, you will be struck dumb until these things come to pass." And he vanished.

Outside the temple, thousands of worshippers were waiting for Zechariah to finish burning the sacred incense and come out of the temple. They waited and waited. Murmurs began to run through the crowd. "Where's the priest? Maybe he's fallen ill. Shouldn't somone go and check? " Elizabeth started to get worried.

Then a shout went up from the people at the front. "Here he comes!" and everyone saw the shape of the elderly priest emerging from the shadows of the temple out into the sunlight. The cheering crowd fell quiet, waiting for Zechariah to speak. Although the priest's lips moved, no sound came out of his mouth. The puzzled men and women looked at each other. What had happened to Zechariah in there? They watched as the priest moved his hands back and forth, silently demonstrating that he had seen a vision from heaven but could no longer speak. The crowd were stunned.

As they stood there, gasping in shock, Elizabeth pushed her way through the throng to her husband's side. And quietly, she led him away from all the fuss.

Not long afterwards, Elizabeth discovered she was expecting a baby. She knew she'd be the talk of the town if people discovered that such an old woman was having a baby. So she tried to keep in the house, out of sight, where she kept her joyous secret to herself. The couple wouldn't let anything spoil their happiness.

Incense shovel
Priests burning incense at the temple used a shovel like this to move burning coals from the altar of burnt offering outside the temple to the smaller incense altar inside.

Altar and incense
The altar for burning incense in the temple was probably this shape, but it would have been made from bronze. It follows the standard pattern, with four horns at the corners on which blood was sprinkled to purify the altar. The incense was made from 13 different ingredients which created smoke – a symbol of the people's prayers going up to heaven.

❖ ABOUT THE STORY ❖

This happy story about a couple having their prayers answered illustrates what the Bible generally teaches about prayer. God did not give them what they asked for just because they were holy people and He thought they deserved it. He answered because the birth of John the Baptist was part of His bigger plan for the world.

A Son for Mary

ABOUT six months after Zechariah's vision in the temple, God sent the angel Gabriel on another important mission. This time his message was for Elizabeth's cousin, Mary.

Mary lived at home with her parents in the region of Galilee, in a town called Nazareth. She was engaged to Joseph, a carpenter who was descended from the great King David, the greatest king of Israel. Every day, as Mary swept and cooked, she looked forward to when she would marry and have a home of her own.

One day, Mary was doing her chores as usual when a light suddenly flooded the room where she was working. She looked up and saw a beautiful man standing in front of her, his face and clothes bright with radiance.

> **You will bear a son, and you shall call His name Jesus.**

"Hello Mary," the man said. "Know that God is with you; I am His messenger, the angel Gabriel. I have come to tell you that the Lord has chosen you above all other women for a very special blessing."

Even though Gabriel had spoken gently, Mary was still petrified. She was always careful to follow God's laws, but she had never expected the Lord to take any notice of a village girl. Priests and elders were far more important than her, and they didn't have angels suddenly appearing in their kitchens.

Gabriel saw the fear on Mary's face.

Nazareth
In Jesus's day Nazareth was a small and obscure town. It was in the north of Judea, overlooking the fertile Plain of Esdraelon. The Church of the Annunciation, on the site where Mary is thought to have seen the angel, is in the centre of the picture.

MARY'S RESPONSE TO THE ANGEL WAS DIFFERENT TO ZECHARIAH'S. SHE DID NOT KNOW HOW IT COULD HAPPEN, BUT HER FAITH WAS FIRM. SHE HAS BEEN A MODEL FOR FAITH EVER SINCE.

Annunciation
When the angel announced to Mary what God intended to do, it was called an annunciation. The event is marked by a service in many churches, on 25 March.

"Don't be afraid," he said, kindly. "God loves you. He's going to send you a son, whom you must call Jesus. He will be ruler over all the Lord's people and His kingdom will have no end."

Poor Mary was even more confused. Nervously, she whispered to the angel, "How can I have a child? I'm not married yet."

"God is going to send His Holy Spirit to you, to grace you with His own Son," the angel replied. "Remember that nothing is impossible for the Lord. Indeed, your cousin Elizabeth has also been blessed and is going to have a baby – even though she's past the age for having children."

Mary was astounded. "How wonderful!" she gasped. As she thought of what the angel promised her she told herself, "It's not right to be afraid, Mary. If the Lord has indeed selected you for this special gift, you should accept it with joy and give thanks for it." With her heart thumping, she said. "I am ready to serve the Lord. Let everything happen to me just as you have said." Gabriel smiled at her and disappeared.

Once the angel had gone, Mary's first thought was to congratulate her cousin. She packed a bag and set off.

Mary couldn't wait to embrace her cousin. "Hello!" she cried as she got closer. "Congratulations!"

As Elizabeth heard her cousin's voice, she felt as if her baby had jumped up inside her to greet Mary. Elizabeth suddenly knew Mary was pregnant, and that the baby would be God's own Son. "Mary, you are the most blessed of all women!" Elizabeth exclaimed, throwing her arms around her. "And what an honour to have the mother of my Lord come to visit me!"

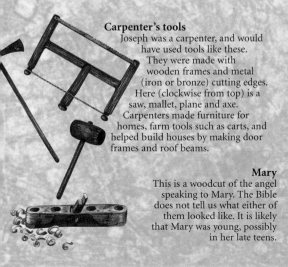

Carpenter's tools
Joseph was a carpenter, and would have used tools like these. They were made with wooden frames and metal (iron or bronze) cutting edges. Here (clockwise from top) is a saw, mallet, plane and axe. Carpenters made furniture for homes, farm tools such as carts, and helped build houses by making door frames and roof beams.

Mary
This is a woodcut of the angel speaking to Mary. The Bible does not tell us what either of them looked like. It is likely that Mary was young, possibly in her late teens.

❖ **ABOUT THE STORY** ❖

The birth of Jesus was carefully planned by God. He decided exactly when, where and how Jesus would be born. Christians see in this story a sign that Jesus really was the Son of God. Because He had no human father but was conceived by the Holy Spirit, Jesus was both fully divine (from His heavenly Father's side) and fully human (from His mother's side).

The Birth of John

MARY stayed with Elizabeth for three months. She was no doubt a great help to her older cousin when she was heavily pregnant with her unborn baby and, of course, the two women shared the amazing secret of how they had each been blessed by the Lord. However, Mary began to worry that she had been away from home too long, and eventually the day came when she sadly told Elizabeth that she must say goodbye. Not long after Mary had gone, her cousin gave birth to a baby boy, just as the angel Gabriel had told Zechariah she would.

Like all proud parents, Elizabeth and Zechariah thought they would burst with happiness. Their friends and relations gathered round to help them celebrate. "What are you going to call him?" someone asked, as they all took turns in cuddling the tiny bundle.

"Oh, they're sure to call him Zechariah after his father," said a family friend, tickling the child under the chin.

"Yes," a relative agreed. "After all, it's the tradition to name him after the father."

"Well maybe they might like to call him after another member of the family," butted in one of the baby's many uncles, while he grabbed the child out of someone else's arms. "For instance, they might like to call him after me!"

"Wait! Wait!" Elizabeth laughed, holding up her hand for silence. She could see that a family argument was about to break out. When everyone was quiet, she said very firmly, "We're going to call him John."

"JOHN!" everyone repeated in shock. "Why ever are you going to call him John?"

The argument began all over again.

"The first boy is always named after his father..."

"There's not a single person in the entire family who's called John..."

Elizabeth stood her ground.

"I'm sorry," she smiled, completely unfussed. "He's going to be called John, and that's that."

❧ ABOUT THE STORY ❧

Names in the Bible were not just labels for people. Often names were given to describe something about them. Jesus was so called because He was 'the Saviour'; His name means 'God saves'. John's name means 'The Lord is gracious', and shows that through him God was preparing to start an important work.

Writing
Most people at this time wrote on a wooden board covered with a layer of wax, which was written on with a stylus, a pointed wooden stick. The wax could later be melted and smoothed over, ready for use again. Parchment and papyrus were too expensive for most people.

Scribes
In biblical times, not everyone could read and write. Scribes were used to write letters and business documents. Their main job, however, was to copy out the religious texts and teach them to the people. They also taught in the schools attached to local synagogues.

She took her baby back into her own arms, where he lay quite content and peaceful.

The relatives and friends wouldn't give up.

"What does Zechariah think?" they urged.

"Surely he can't be happy about this John business?" Elizabeth sighed.

"Why don't you ask him yourself?" she suggested.

Everyone looked at each other, slightly embarrassed.

"He might not be able to speak," Elizabeth said loudly, getting a little red in the face, "but he hasn't lost the ability to think or write."

66 *He shall be called John.* 99

The friends and relations found a writing tablet and a pen, and crowded round the elderly priest in anticipation.

"WHAT DO YOU WANT HIM TO BE CALLED?" one of them yelled in Zechariah's face.

"He's not deaf either, you know," Elizabeth murmured.

Slowly and carefully, in big, clear letters, Zechariah wrote out 'His name is John'.

There was utter commotion as the relatives and friends read Zechariah's words.

"Well, I don't believe it!" one remarked.

"John!" another spluttered. "John!"

"Yes," said Zechariah, above the hubbub. "His name is John." There was a gasp of astonishment as all heads turned to look at the priest. His eyes widened and he clapped his hands over his mouth in surprise. "I can talk!" he whispered. "My voice has come back!" he shouted.

"Thanks be to God!" And he grabbed hold of the laughing Elizabeth and whirled her round, dancing and singing.

After that, there wasn't a single person in the whole of the hill country of Judea who didn't get to hear of the child who had been born so late to Elizabeth and Zechariah, and the miracle of how the priest's voice had returned. Everyone knew that the Lord must have had a hand in the amazing events, and they waited in awe to see what kind of man the child would grow up to be.

Jewish motifs

Jesus was born and raised as a Jew, and worshipped in the Jewish synagogue. This mosaic depicts several Jewish motifs. In the centre is the seven-branched candlestick (the menorah). Also shown here is a shofar (a ram's horn, bottom right) which priests blew to mark the start of the Sabbath and other holy days. Above it is an incense shovel.

Benedictine faith

When Zechariah could speak again, he uttered a prophetic poem about the ministry of his son John. This poem is called the Benedictus, and is still sung in some church services today. Later, Saint Benedict founded the Benedictine order of monks and nuns, shown here.

The Birth of Jesus

WHEN Mary told Joseph that she was expecting a baby, he was very worried. They weren't yet married and there was sure to be a scandal. That night, Joseph had a vivid dream. An angel said, "Joseph, don't be afraid to take Mary as your wife. The baby growing within her is the Son of God. He is the Saviour who the prophets said would one day come to save everyone from their sins. When the child is born, call Him Jesus. Raise Him as if He were your own son." Joseph awoke much comforted.

As the time drew near for the baby to be born, another problem arose. The Emperor Augustus Caesar ordered a census. This meant that very man had to go to where he was born, together with his family, to be put on a register.

Joseph had to travel to Bethlehem, a long way from Nazareth. Mary was heavily pregnant. It was not a good time for her to be travelling.

By the time they arrived, the city was full to bursting. There wasn't a single room to be had. Joseph and Mary trudged from place to place, exhausted, dirty and starving. And Mary began to feel that the baby was on its way.

Bang! Joseph thumped on the door of an inn.

"We haven't any room," said the burly innkeeper from behind the door.

"Wait!" Joseph yelled. "Please! We just need a tiny corner somewhere, somewhere warm and dry. It doesn't matter where. My wife's about to give birth!"

> 66 *She wrapped Him in swaddling cloths, and laid Him in a manger.* 99

The innkeeper said, a little more gently, "All my rooms are completely full. I can offer you the stable, if you don't mind the animals. You're welcome to stay there if you like."

Augustus
The Emperor who ruled at this time was Augustus. Originally called Octavian, he was given the name Augustus when he became the first emperor of Rome, in 27 BC. He was a great administrator, and ordered several censuses. His aim was to govern the entire empire from Europe to Judea firmly but fairly.

JOSEPH DID WHAT GOD WANTED, BUT HE HAD TO DO WHAT THE AUTHORITIES WANTED TOO. GOD MADE SURE THAT DESPITE THE EMPEROR'S ORDERS, HIS SON WOULD BE BORN SAFELY.

Mary, mother of Jesus
The Bible tells us very little about the Virgin Mary. Like Joseph, she was descended from David. Many Christians believe that she remained a virgin throughout her life. She is regarded as the most important of all the saints.

Joseph accepted the offer gratefully, so it was in the innkeeper's stable, with the oxen, sheep and chickens looking on, that the Saviour of the world was born. Mary had no crib in which to lay her precious bundle, so she nestled Him among the straw of a manger from which the animals fed. There the baby Jesus stayed. He was safe and warm and sheltered, and He had His loving mother and father at His side.

Joseph

In New Testament times an engagement between two people was regarded as binding as marriage itself. The only way to break it was to get a divorce. It was also thought to be sinful if someone had a sexual relationship before they were married. So Joseph probably thought Mary had been unfaithful to him. The angel told him it was a miracle, and so he loved Mary and cared for her.

❖ ABOUT THE STORY ❖

The story of Jesus's birth is very moving. It reveals important truths about God's plans for the world. Jesus was born in a borrowed room, not in a king's palace, even though He was the 'King of kings' before whom everyone should bow in honour. It teaches that Jesus came into the world to show God's love for people who feel they have nothing. God has known the same sadness as they know.

The Visit of the Shepherds

WHILE Bethlehem was full to bursting with people, the fields around the city were quiet and empty, except for a few shepherds and their flocks. As usual, the men were spending the night under the starry sky, taking turns at sleeping and watching, so that no sheep would go astray, stolen by wolves or even bears. It was a cold and lonely job. They had only the dying flames of the campfire to keep them warm. Apart from its flickering, and the pale glow of the moon and stars, all was calm, all was still.

Suddenly the night sky above blazed as if it were on fire. It was like trying to look into the full glare of the

Praising God
In churches today, a choir sings hymns, psalms and songs as part of worshipping God. Music is a powerful way of praising God. The pictures of heaven given in the Bible describe angels and people singing God's praises.

CLUB

CROOK

BOWL

A shepherd's tools
These are the tools a shepherd would have used. The club was for fighting off attacking wolves. He also had a food bowl from which he could eat. The crook was used for rescuing lost sheep.

A shepherd's cloak
Sheepskins would have been made into warm coats. These were to keep shepherds warm as they stayed up to guard their shee

scorching desert sun. The shepherds fell back, trying to shield their eyes as high overhead a figure appeared.

"Do not be afraid," came its voice, speaking clearly into the mind of each of the shepherds. "I have news that will bring great joy to everyone on earth. Today in Bethlehem, the city of David, a Saviour has been born who is Christ, the Lord. You will find Him wrapped up in swaddling clothes and lying in a manger."

> " *To you is born this day a Saviour, who is Christ the Lord.* "

The sound of countless singing voices filled the air. The heavens were filled with angels.

"Glory to God in the highest," they sang, "and peace to His people on earth."

Then suddenly the singing died away and the light faded. The dazed shepherds were left staring up at the sky. The gleaming moon and stars now seemed only an echo of the real beauty of the heavens, which they had glimpsed for a while and had now disappeared.

The shepherds hurried off to Bethlehem, leaving only a couple of men behind to guard the flocks. They were excited. The prophets had spoken of a Christ, or Messiah, whom God would send to save the world from its sins. Had this most amazing person now been born?

The shepherds searched from place to place in the packed town until they heard the crying of an infant coming from a stable behind an inn. The shepherds found Mary and Joseph huddled over the manger, attending to a baby wrapped in swaddling clothes.

"It is indeed the Saviour! Christ, the Lord!" the shepherds gasped, approaching the little family and falling on their knees. They told the startled parents about the visit from the angels and what they had said. When the shepherds had paid their tributes and gone, singing praises to God as they went, Mary and Joseph began to wonder and marvel at everything that had happened.

Medieval nativity
Many pictures have been painted of the first Christmas. This one shows the shepherds together with the wise men. Mary and Jesus have haloes round their heads. Artists used this device to show people who were specially blessed by God.

✦ ABOUT THE STORY ✦

Shepherds were despised by most people. They were thought to be liars and couldn't give evidence in court. Only people with no hope could be shepherds. This story reminds readers that God has shown Himself specially to people who everyone else despises and who think they are not good enough for God. The good news of Christianity is for everyone, regardless of background.

Jesus is Presented in the Temple

WHEN their baby was eight days old, Mary held a naming ceremony according to God's laws. From then on, the baby was called Jesus, just as the angel had told Mary He should be. Then, according to the custom, Mary and Joseph travelled up from Bethlehem to the temple in Jerusalem to present Jesus to the Lord and to offer a sacrifice of two doves or pigeons.

Now there lived in Jerusalem an old man whose name was Simeon. Simeon had always done his best to lead a good life and was well known by everyone in the city to be a very holy man. As the people of Jerusalem watched him make his way to and from the temple every day, his lips moving in constant prayer, they never dreamed that he had a precious secret. The Holy Spirit had promised Simeon that, as a reward for his faithful, lifelong service to God, he would not die before he had seen with his own eyes the Messiah who would save the world. Simeon felt he had been blessed with the highest of honours, and he looked forward with his whole heart to the moment that he would meet his Saviour.

> ❝ *Mine eyes have seen thy salvation which thou hast prepared in the presence of all peoples.* ❞

When Mary and Joseph arrived in the temple with Jesus, Simeon was already there. That morning, the Holy Spirit had once again spoken to him, telling him that

❧ ABOUT THE STORY ❧

To most people, Jesus was just another baby. To those who were trying to look at the world through the eyes of faith, He was someone special. Even today, some people, like Simeon and Anna, are gifted with a kind of spiritual second sight that helps them to discern God's purposes behind events. They are called prophets. This event helped Mary and Joseph to know more about Jesus.

Mary weeps
When Mary took Jesus to the temple, Simeon prophesied that she would suffer much grief because of what would happen to Jesus.

Taking Jesus to the temple
The Jewish law said that after 40 days a woman who had a son must offer a sacrifice at the temple. The proper sacrifice was a lamb and a pigeon, but poor people were allowed to bring two pigeons. The ceremony dates back to Old Testament times when eldest sons used to have to become priests. Then when the Levites took this role, the Israelites would symbolically 'buy back' their sons from God, from the priesthood, by making a sacrifice as Mary does here

today was the great day when God's promise to him would be fulfilled. With his heart pounding in his breast, Simeon had prepared himself with great haste and hurried to the temple as fast as he could. And as soon as the old man laid eyes on the baby, he knew who He was.

"May God almighty bless you," Simeon cried, holding out his trembling arms to hold the child. "I have long dreamt about this day. Now I can die in peace, for my eyes have seen the one who will save the world. This child will be the glory of Israel and the light of hope for all the peoples of the earth."

Simeon turned to the stunned parents. "This child is a sign from God, but many will not listen to His message," the old man said to Mary. "Because of this, a great sadness will pierce through your heart like a sword," he continued. "However, He will also win many hearts for the Lord."

While Simeon was speaking, a woman even older than Simeon shuffled up. It was Anna, the prophetess. She had spent much of her life in the temple, devoting herself to fasting and prayer.

"Allow me the blessing of holding my Saviour," she said. A curious crowd was beginning to gather around the family and Anna lifted her voice aloud, thanking God for allowing her to see the holy child and telling everyone that the infant was the hope of the world.

As soon as Mary and Joseph had made their offering, they said goodbye to Simeon and Anna and hurried away from the eyes of the temple worshippers. They were more than a little embarrassed by all the fuss, and naturally felt bewildered by the strangeness of everything that had happened since their son's birth.

Simeon and Anna
Simeon and Anna were people of faith who were expecting God to do something special. They didn't know what to expect, but prompted by the Holy Spirit they recognized Jesus.

The journey
The distance from Nazareth to Bethlehem was about 129km. Mary and Joseph walked there. It does not say in the Bible that Mary rode on a donkey, but it is quite likely that she would have done. There were well-trodden tracks between towns, but no paved roads. Bethlehem was a short distance from where the temple was in Jerusalem.

The Wise Men Find Jesus

FAR away in the east, some learned priests were puzzled to see that a strange star suddenly appeared one night in the sky. Not only was it a star they had never noticed before, but it shone brighter than any other. The wise men hurried off to consult their writings. They agreed that the brilliant star was an unmistakable sign. The saviour had been born. Now all they had to do was find Him.

The wise men spread out their maps and plotted a route from the position of the star. Finally, they chose

gifts for the child who was King of the whole earth. Then they mounted their camels and set off across the desert.

News reached King Herod that strangers from the orient were searching Jerusalem. "They're looking for a child that has been born king of the Jews," the king's spies told him.

"Are they, indeed?" murmured Herod, stroking his beard thoughtfully. After all, he was king of the Jews. Somewhere in Judea, a rebellion was brewing. He kept calm and summoned the chief priests and scribes to a meeting. Herod pretended that he was curious to learn more.

"Where do your scriptures say that the Christ child is to be born?" Herod asked innocently.

"The prophets say that the Messiah will be born in Bethlehem," the priests replied.

Herod nodded, interestedly. He had the answer that he needed.

As soon as the priests and scribes had gone, the king called for the most trusted officers in his army.

"Find these wise men from the east," he ordered, "and bring them to me. Only do it in secret, or the people will really start to take notice of these rumours."

Soon, the wise men were ushered into the presence of the king of Judea. They had heard that Herod was a ruthless, harsh ruler and were worried. However, Herod was politeness itself.

"When exactly did this star appear?" the king asked. The wise men told him all they knew about the child.

The magi
Most pictures show three wise men, or magi, because they brought three gifts, although this number is not used in the Bible. It is likely that there were more than three as people tended to travel in larger groups. They were learned priests, not kings as is sometimes suggested.

Astrologers
The magi were also astrologers. In ancient times, astronomy (the study of stars and planets) and astrology (giving advice based on this) were practised by the same people. The Jews were not to use astrology – God alone was their guide.

The wise men did indeed find Jesus in Bethlehem. The star shone biggest and brightest over the town and led the travellers to where Mary and Joseph were now staying. They were surprised at the arrival of the splendidly dressed guests, just as the wise men were to find the holy family in an ordinary house. They had no doubt, though, that the baby was the king of all kings. They bowed their heads to the floor and paid tribute, then they unlocked their jewelled caskets and offered Mary their gifts of gold, rarest frankincense and myrrh.

The night before the wise men set off on their return, they had a dream which deeply disturbed them. "Herod must not be told," they agreed. They took a different route home, so that the evil king could not find them.

In turn, Herod seemed most helpful.

"Try Bethlehem instead of Jerusalem," he suggested.

The wise men bowed down and thanked Herod for his generous help. There was no time to waste.

"Oh, by the way," Herod added, "when you have found the child, would you be so kind as to tell me where He is? I must of course go and worship Him myself."

> ❝ *They offered Him gifts, gold and frankincense and myrrh.* ❞

"Consider it done, O King," the wise men agreed.

As soon as the door closed behind them, Herod thumped his fist down on his throne.

"As soon as I know where this 'king' is, I will make sure He is killed!" he snarled.

Casket and gifts
The gifts brought by the magi may have been in a casket like this. The gold was the sign of royalty, frankincense was a sign for a priest and myrrh was a sign of death and burial.

Arabia
This is the town of San'aa in Yemen, in Arabia. The Bible tells us that the magi came from the east. The most likely places are Arabia and Babylon.

❖ **ABOUT THE STORY** ❖

The wise men were gentiles (non-Jews). Their appearance in only Matthew's gospel is of great significance to Christians. The message is that Jesus has come into the world for all peoples. Matthew, in fact, is the most Jewish of the gospels so this story is a reminder of Jesus's wider ministry. This event is celebrated in many churches as the Feast of Epiphany (6 January).

Escape to Egypt

MARY and Joseph marvelled at how far the wise men had travelled to see their son. So many strange things had happened since He had been born. Maybe the departure of the wise men would mark an end to all the amazing and unusual events for a while...

That night, Joseph once again dreamt that an angel came and stood by his side.

"You must take Mary and the baby and hurry away from here at once," came the angel's urgent message. "Flee into Egypt and stay there until I come to tell you it is safe to return. King Herod of Judea is going to search for the child. He is determined to kill Him."

Next morning, Joseph gently shook Mary awake and told her to get Jesus ready. He lifted his wife and her precious child onto the donkey and the family crept away unnoticed through the quiet streets of Bethlehem.

Meanwhile, in Jerusalem, King Herod was waiting for the wise men to return. Every day, he grew more and more frustrated and more and more angry.

"Surely those wretched astrologers must have found the child by now?" he'd bellow at his trembling advisers.

The days turned into weeks, and still Herod grew more and more furious. Finding his rival, the baby Christ, was top of his agenda. The thunder-faced king could think of nothing else. How could he enjoy life, knowing that rumours were spreading about another king of the Jews? Besides, if the wise men were right, and this baby really was the Messiah spoken of in the scriptures, He would soon have supporters up and down the country. And that would leave Herod at serious risk of losing his throne.

One sunset, as yet another day ended with no word from the wise men, King Herod finally snapped. "Bring me the general of the royal army!" he howled with rage.

The burly army commander was at once ushered in.

"Order your men to go through every single household in the Bethlehem area and find every male child under two years old," Herod spat, "then kill them all."

A gasp went around the court room.

The blood drained from the general's face and he fell to his knees before the ruthless, cruel monarch.

"But... but... sire, surely..." he stuttered, falling silent as Herod bent down to whisper in his ear.

"If I hear that there is even one male child under two years old left alive, I shall hold you personally responsible," hissed the king, and he swept away to his private chambers, leaving the army general grovelling miserably on the cold palace floor.

> 66 *Herod is about to search for the child, to destroy Him.* 99

Soon, the sound of screaming rose up over Bethlehem. No one could escape the heartbreaking shrieks that tore the air. Panicking parents ran desperately to and fro, trying to secret away their tiny sons. The soldiers marched like machines into every possible hiding place. They trampled over those who threw themselves to the ground and begged for them to have mercy. They turned deaf ears to pleading and crying of men and women beside themselves with grief.

At last, when there was not a single male child under the age of two left in the whole of the area around Bethlehem, Herod was satisfied. So much then for the supposed Messiah, king of the Jews!

In fact Jesus was long gone. Joseph kept Him and His mother safe in Egypt until the angel told him that Herod had died and it was time to return home to Judea. So finally the family returned to the quiet town of Nazareth in the remote district of Galilee, where Jesus grew up far away from the evil eyes of Herod's son, King Archelaus.

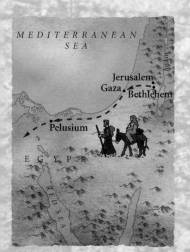

THE FACT THAT JESUS EVENTUALLY RETURNS TO ISRAEL, FROM EGYPT, TO SAVE THE PEOPLE THERE ECHOES THE WAY THAT THE ISRAELITES FLED EGYPT WITH MOSES HUNDREDS OF YEARS BEFORE.

Flight into Egypt
The gospel of Matthew tells us that as soon as Joseph was told by the angel that Jesus was in danger he took his family out of Israel to Egypt. It was a long and difficult trip for the family to make, especially as Jesus was so young.

❖ ABOUT THE STORY ❖

Herod the Great is known to have been a violent and cruel man, who was greatly afraid of rivals. He even had two of his own sons put on trial, convicted and executed because of an alleged family plot against him. There is no record outside the New Testament of this event (which was confined to Bethlehem), but it would be typical of Herod to order it.

Lost and Found

IN the sleepy town of Nazareth, Jesus grew up just like all the other children. Mary and Joseph taught Him to obey all the laws of their religion and made sure that He learned all the teachings of the holy scriptures.

Every year, Mary and Joseph travelled to Jerusalem to celebrate the great festival of Passover, as all Jews tried to do. One year, when Jesus was 12 years old, the family went as usual to share the wonderful experience of praising God in the temple at this important time of the year.

When it was time to go home, Mary and Joseph found a crowd of travellers planning to go their way. Jesus disappeared among them. Like all children His age, He

didn't want to walk by His parents' side. He wanted to talk with His own friends. Mary and Joseph weren't worried. They knew their son was sensible enough to keep close by.

After the first day's journey, when the tired, dusty travellers were getting ready to make camp for the night, Jesus was nowhere to be seen.

"Jesus! Jesus!" called Mary and Joseph, at the tops of their voices. The boy didn't come running.

The anxious couple hurried from group to group.

"Has anyone seen our son?" they asked. "He has very dark eyes; He's about this high; He's very gentle and well-mannered; a quiet, thoughtful boy."

Everyone just shook their heads.

Joseph looked very serious. Mary was close to tears.

"There's nothing more we can do now," the carpenter told his wife, putting his arm around her. "First thing in the morning, we'll retrace our steps."

Neither Mary nor Joseph managed to sleep for worry. Anything could have happened to Jesus. What if He had been kidnapped by bandits or eaten by wild animals? It didn't bear thinking about.

> **❝** *All who heard Him were amazed at His understanding and His answers.* **❞**

As they went back to Jerusalem, Jesus's parents grew more anxious. There wasn't a single sign as to what had happened to Him. The boy had just disappeared.

People milled everywhere in the narrow streets, jostling

Herod's temple
This was the greatest of all three temples which had been built in Jerusalem. Herod began it in 20BC. It was opened in 9BC but not actually finished until AD64. As a boy, Jesus could go into the first two of the three courtyards, the Court of Gentiles and the Court of the Women. At 13, like any Jewish man, He could go into the Court of Israel. But no one except priests could go inside the main building. Around the courtyards were stores and offices, and covered passages.

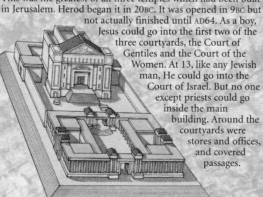

Bar and Bat Mitzvah
When Jewish girls reach the age of 12 they have their Bat Mitzvah, Jewish boys have a Bar Mitzvah aged 13. This is a ceremony when in the eyes of their religion, they become adults, and take on the religious duties of a Jewish adult.

was going on in one of the porticoes. They could see elders and priests, deep in discussion. They tiptoed forwards. Then Mary's voice rang out loud and clear.

"Jesus!" she gasped, pushing her way through the learned men to where Jesus stood in the middle of them.

"Please excuse us," Joseph explained. "We've been looking for Him all over the place."

To his utter astonishment, the leaders all shook his hand.

"We cannot believe your son's understanding of the scriptures," they told him. "And He has raised searching questions that few people ask."

Meanwhile, Mary's relief at finding her son was giving way to anger.

"Jesus, we have been worried sick!" she scolded. "How could you just go off on your own and leave your father and me wondering where you were?"

"You should have known that you would find me in my Father's house," Jesus said, calmly.

Mary was taken aback at Jesus's strange answer, but she didn't have the time to puzzle over His mysterious words. All she wanted to do now was get back home safely. Later, she remembered Jesus's strange reply. And, of course, she hadn't forgotten the angel, the shepherds and the wise men, Simeon and Anna in the temple. It was all very mysterious indeed...

shoulder to shoulder. It was looking like an impossible task. Several times they thought they saw Jesus, and several times it turned out to be another boy about His age. They couldn't leave without their precious son. They would hunt high and low until they found Him, hopefully alive and well. By the third day the only place the desperate parents hadn't searched was the great temple itself.

Wearily, Mary and Joseph climbed the great stone steps and entered the huge courtyard. Some type of meeting

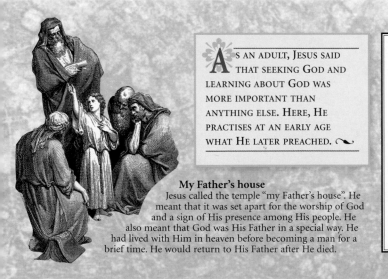

AS AN ADULT, JESUS SAID THAT SEEKING GOD AND LEARNING ABOUT GOD WAS MORE IMPORTANT THAN ANYTHING ELSE. HERE, HE PRACTISES AT AN EARLY AGE WHAT HE LATER PREACHED.

My Father's house

Jesus called the temple "my Father's house". He meant that it was set apart for the worship of God and a sign of His presence among His people. He also meant that God was His Father in a special way. He had lived with Him in heaven before becoming a man for a brief time. He would return to His Father after He died.

❖ ABOUT THE STORY ❖

We know little about Jesus' boyhood, and nothing about how He looked or how He behaved. Some legends were made up in the 3rd and 4th centuries, but none of them can be traced any earlier. This story shows that Jesus was aware of His special relationship with God from an early age. It also shows that He learned to obey His parents in His preparation to obey God.

Jesus is Baptized

JESUS'S cousin, John, grew up to devote his life entirely to God. When he was a young man, he went off on his own into the wilderness around the River Jordan. John just wrapped a rough camel skin around him and ate locusts and honeycombs that he found in the wild.

When John was around 30 years old, a change came upon him. Instead of keeping himself to himself, he began to preach to all the peoples who lived near the river.

"I have heard the word of God!" he would yell. "You must think about your sins and be truly sorry for them. I

hear you say that you're Abraham's descendants, God's chosen people. I tell you that God could raise these very stones up to life, if He wanted. Beg the Lord's forgiveness and be good. For the day is coming when the Lord will judge sinners."

> ❝ *I have baptized you with water; but He will baptize you with the Holy Spirit.* ❞

People began to travel to the Jordan to hear what John had to say. All kinds of men and women came, common folk, noblemen, priests, tax collectors, even Roman soldiers. No matter who they were, John's message was the same. He said people should turn back to God, be kind, don't cheat or lie, and don't hurt anybody with harsh words or violence.

Every day, people would line up by the River Jordan, eager to be forgiven for their wrongdoings and wanting to make a new start. One by one, John would take them into the river and submerge them, blessing them as they rose up from the water a Christian.

As the weeks passed, rumours began to spread among the people of Galilee.

"Maybe this John is the Messiah spoken of by the prophets..." people would murmur.

"Surely this holy man is the Christ!" exclaimed others.

John was always very clear about the truth.

❧ ABOUT THE STORY ❧

This event marks the beginning of Jesus's public ministry. Through it He received confirmation that He was indeed the Son of God, and He received the spiritual power He needed to do His work. His baptism was also a way of identifying with the people He came to die for. He was saying that He was willing to take people's sin on His shoulders, which He did on the cross.

Baptism
Baptism is a ceremony in which a person is submerged beneath water, or sprinkled with water, as a sign that they want to follow Jesus and turn away from their sins. Most churches use it as the main ceremony to make someone a church member.

John
We do not know where John grew up. It seems possible that his parents, Zechariah and Elizabeth, died when he was young, and that he grew up in a religious community in the desert. His work was foretold in the Old Testament, and he was likened to Elijah. Here you can see John baptizing Jesus.

"I am not the Messiah, or Elijah, or any other prophet. I am merely one voice crying out in the wilderness, trying to prepare the way for the Lord," he said. "I'm baptizing you with water, but there is one coming soon who will baptize you with the fire of the Holy Spirit. He is much greater than me – so great that I'm not even fit for the job of cleaning His sandals."

When Jesus himself arrived among the crowds at the banks of the Jordan, John knew who He was immediately, and he told everyone who was there.

"Here He comes!" he cried, falling on his knees. "The one God has promised us! The one who will take away the sins of all the world!"

Jesus laid a hand gently on his cousin's arm and looked deep into his eyes.

"Will you baptize me too, John?" He asked.

"My lord," John gasped. "I can't baptize you! It should be you who baptizes me!"

However, Jesus insisted.

"We should each of us do what God has given us to do," He said, quietly.

And so John led Jesus down into the Jordan.

At the very moment that John blessed Jesus as He rose from the waters, the two men heard a mighty thunderclap. John looked up to see the clouds of the heavens parting, and a dove came gliding down bathed in heavenly light. John knew that the Holy Spirit was descending on his cousin. Then a voice spoke that seemed to come from everywhere and nowhere all at once.

"This is my beloved Son," the voice said, "with whom I am well pleased."

Locusts and honey

Locusts are large grasshoppers which can breed into great swarms. They are very nutritious and are still eaten today. Wild bees made nests in rocky places. John could collect their honey.

Sadducees

Most Sadducees were priests, but not all priests were Sadducees. They were a group within Judaism. As a group they were very snobbish and mostly came from the upper classes. They despised ordinary people. In Jesus's time, they were the major group in the Sanhedrin, the Jews' ruling council. However, they often had to follow the Pharisees because the latter were popular with the ordinary people. They accepted only the written laws of the Old Testament, and not all the extra ones the Pharisees made up. They did not believe in life after death, or that God could or would guide a person's life. The Sadducees died out after the temple was destroyed by the Romans in AD70. No one is sure how they started, whether as a political, religious or aristocratic group.

Tempted in the Wilderness

JESUS knew He was the Son of God, the Messiah the prophets had said would come to save the world from its sins. Now He had to prepare for the job He had been sent to do.

Led by the Holy Spirit, Jesus went into the wilderness where He could be on His own to pray. There He talked to God for 40 days and 40 nights, asking for guidance in the difficult days that lay ahead. He ate nothing, and as Jesus grew weak with hunger and exhaustion, the devil came to Him in His thoughts.

"If you really are the Son of God," Satan whispered, "why don't you turn these stones into bread?"

Jesus knew this would be wrong on several counts. First, He had heard the voice of the Lord calling Him His Son. He knew He should have faith that this was true, not try to work a miracle to prove it. Second, eating was far less important than obeying God. Jesus realized that His body would die if He didn't eat, but His body would die one day anyway. It was far more important to look after His soul by not doing anything that would offend His Father in heaven. Besides, He should trust God to look after Him. After all, long ago, Moses had led the starving Israelites through the desert. He had trusted the Lord, and God had sent them food from heaven.

Jesus summoned up His strength.

"No," He told the devil. "People can't live on bread alone; we need to listen to the words of God to survive."

Satan was annoyed. However, he tried not to let it show. Instead, he put a picture of the holy city of Jerusalem in Jesus's mind. It was as if Jesus was standing right on the top of the great temple, looking down on the streets and houses all around. Balancing so high up made Jesus dizzy and His head began to whirl and spin.

"If you really are the Son of God," Satan challenged, "don't be afraid to fall off. The angels will come and catch you. They'll make sure you don't even bruise a single toe."

It was a very tempting thought. Why struggle to do things the hard way, fighting Satan, when there was a quick solution? Jesus knew it would be wrong. His life as the Messiah was going to be dangerous, sad and lonely. There would be no easy way out. His Father in heaven wanted Him to live as a human, to show people the right way to God – even if it was the most difficult way of all.

✦ ABOUT THE STORY ✦

Jesus was tempted in the same way as everyone else. The first temptation was to put the satisfaction of His own needs and desires before God's will. The second was to take a short cut to do God's work, rather than do it in God's way. The third was to grab power over people for Himself. The message is that we should not just be concerned with the end result, but also how we get there.

The Judean Desert
This area is wild and inhospitable. There are oases (for water), but it is hot in the day and cold at night, and there is little shelter. Jesus was here about six weeks. The desert is often thought of as a place of testing because it is a place of extremes.

JESUS RESISTED TEMPTATION BY QUOTING FROM GOD'S WORD, WHICH IS A GOOD WAY OF DEALING WITH IT. IF THOUGHTS AGREE WITH THE BIBLE, THEY ARE FROM GOD; IF NOT, THEY COME FROM THE DEVIL. ∾

wonders of the world. Images of golden palaces, splendid temples and treasure houses overflowing with all the riches of the earth arose in Jesus's mind. There were magnificent armies of brave-hearted warriors and rows of gleaming chariots led by prancing horses. There were fleets of ships laden with exotic cargoes from mysterious lands...

"Take a good look!" urged Satan. "All this can be yours. I will give it all to you – if only you will bow down and worship me."

Jesus knew that the devil was indeed mighty, for he had hold of many people's hearts. Those who turned to Satan to make them powerful ended up cruel, dishonest and selfish. They ruled by crushing others, and kept themselves happy by making others miserable. Those who followed the Lord might not become rich or famous, but they would find love and happiness and be truly at peace.

> 66 *You shall worship the Lord your God, and Him only shall you serve.* 99

"No," He told the devil, firmly. "It is wrong to put God to the test like this. The easiest thing to do is by no means always the best."

Satan was furious, but he didn't give up. Instead, he whisked Jesus's thoughts away to the highest mountain in the world. As if Jesus were an eagle, flying high up in the skies, He could see the whole earth spread out below Him. How beautiful His Father had created everything! Waving fields of crops grew out of pink and brown soil. Wide carpets of green grass and sweet-smelling forests covered plains and hills. Deserts glowed yellow and ice caps shone blue-white. Rivers rippled and sparkled down to seas as broad as the skies above. The devil showed Jesus all the

Besides which, Jesus knew that all kingdoms of the world will one day fade to dust and that only the kingdom of God will last for ever.

"No," He told the devil, in disgust. "Get away from me! People should worship only the Lord God."

Satan nearly exploded with frustration. He had tempted Jesus with all he had. Raging wildly, the devil disappeared. And as Jesus sank down in the sands of the desert, utterly worn out, angels came to look after Him.

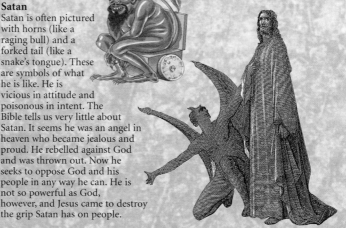

Satan
Satan is often pictured with horns (like a raging bull) and a forked tail (like a snake's tongue). These are symbols of what he is like. He is vicious in attitude and poisonous in intent. The Bible tells us very little about Satan. It seems he was an angel in heaven who became jealous and proud. He rebelled against God and was thrown out. Now he seeks to oppose God and his people in any way he can. He is not so powerful as God, however, and Jesus came to destroy the grip Satan has on people.

The First Miracle

JESUS left Judea and travelled back to Galilee. It was time to begin teaching the people what they had to do to enter the kingdom of God. Several of John the Baptist's followers went along with Jesus, wanting to help. As soon as Jesus arrived home, He and His mother had to go to a wedding in Cana. Weddings were always big, important celebrations and often lasted several days.

Perhaps the steward in charge of the wedding reception hadn't ordered enough wine for such a large feast. Or maybe the guests were drinking more than usual. Whatever the reason, Mary noticed halfway through the wedding reception that the wine had almost run out. While the guests were all munching and slurping their way through each delicious course, nervous, red-faced servants were scurrying off with empty wine jars.

"Look. There's no more wine left," Mary quietly said to her son.

Jesus was concerned. He knew how embarrassing it would be for the bride and groom if they had nothing to offer their thirsty guests to drink.

"I'm sorry, but I can't do anything about it," He whispered back. "The time is not yet right for me to show the powers my Father has given me."

Mary just held His hand and nodded, reassuringly. Then she turned to the servants nearby.

"Excuse me," she said, politely. "I couldn't help noticing that you're almost out of wine. My son can help you. Just do exactly as He says."

Jesus looked at His beloved mother and smiled. Then with a sigh, He said to the servants, "Fill your empty jars up to the brim with water."

66 *The steward of the feast tasted the water now become wine.* 99

Very puzzled, they hurried off to carry out his instructions. And soon they were back, struggling under the weight of their full urns.

"Now draw out some of the water into a goblet," Jesus told them, "and take it to the steward for tasting." (It was the custom for the steward to check every jar that came out of the cellar, to make sure that the wine was good.)

Well, the servants were mystified. They were sure that their boss would think they had gone mad when they took him water to test, pretending it was wine. They didn't dare refuse to carry out one of the guest's instructions. And besides, there was something about the man's kind eyes and His mother's gentle manner that made them trust that everything would be all right.

Now the steward was an expert wine taster. And he knew all the tricks of

Cana
This was a small village north of Nazareth. We are not sure of the exact site today. The town pictured may be built near it.

Water jars
Water jars were usually used for the ceremonial washing of people's feet. It was the custom to wash a visitor's feet when they came to your house; they wore open sandals. Many Jews also insisted on ritual washings before they ate, as a religious act.

his trade, such as serving the best wine first and bringing out the cheaper wine later, when the guests were less aware of what they were drinking. So when he drank this time from the servant's goblet, he was amazed. This new wine was even better than the wine they had served at first! Before the servants could explain where it had come from, the steward hurried off to congratulate the groom on his good taste and generosity.

Jesus had worked the first of many miracles He was to perform throughout His life. His followers had seen Him do the impossible, and they believed more strongly than ever that He truly was the Son of God.

ARY'S WORDS – "DO EXACTLY AS HE SAYS" – ARE ADVICE WHICH EVERYONE CAN FOLLOW. IN ORDER TO LIVE IN GOD'S WAY, CHRISTIANS BELIEVE THAT WE HAVE TO DO EVERYTHING HE SAYS.

Wine tasting
This shows the steward tasting the wine. Wine in the New Testament can also stand for Jesus's blood, which He shed on the cross for the sins of the world. It is significant that Jesus's first miracle involved wine, as if looking forward to His greater miracle of salvation.

ABOUT THE STORY

Jesus sometimes said that His teaching was like new wine, or that He came to bring to people the new wine of the kingdom of God. He meant that He brought the new life of the Holy Spirit to people who would follow Him. As with many of His teachings, Jesus illustrated His words by His miracles. God's new life is plentiful, like the supply of wine at Cana. There is plenty of it.

Followers Flock to Jesus

JESUS began to travel around Galilee, teaching from synagogue to synagogue.

"Beg the Lord to forgive your sins," He urged, just like His cousin John the Baptist. "For the time is near when the doors of God's kingdom will be thrown open. The Holy Spirit has sent me to bring the good news that captives will be set free, the blind will see and the poor will no longer have to suffer."

Everyone who heard Jesus was amazed at the way He spoke. He didn't simply read out the scriptures, as other scribes did. He interpreted them as if He were sure He knew what they were all about.

Jesus's actions were pretty astounding too. Jesus was preaching one day in Capernaum, when a madman suddenly flew into a crazy fit.

"I know who you are," the madman yelled at Jesus. "You're the Holy One of God! What do you want with us? Have you come here to destroy us all?"

Jesus remained calm. He said firmly, "Be quiet!" He stared at the madman. "Leave him!" He commanded.

At once, the man crumpled into a heap on the floor. At Jesus's command, the demons left him.

❧ ABOUT THE STORY ❧

There was something "different" about Jesus. It was not just what He said nor was it just what He did – there had been miracle workers before. He was in a class apart, and people could see it. However, He wouldn't explain it. Jesus silenced the one person who really knew – the madman. He wanted people to learn to trust Him in the ordinary things of life.

The miraculous catch of fish
This had a special impact on Peter. He knew that fish went to the bottom of the lake in the daytime, where the water was cooler. If Jesus had the power to make the fish come into the net, He could do anything. The miracle spoke to Peter in terms he understood.

The worshippers were left in shock.

"Who on earth is this man?" they whispered.

Reports spread like wildfire about what had happened. Even though it was nearly dark, everyone who heard about the captivating stranger with the special powers came at once to find Him. Sick and injured people came flooding from the nearby towns and villages to be healed by Jesus.

> " *I know who you are, the Holy One of God.* "

He laid His hands on them, filling them with a sense of forgiveness and hope, curing each and every disease.

"You will stay with us, won't you?" the people pleaded.

"I'm afraid I can't," Jesus explained. "I must move on to other places. I have to tell everyone how they can find happiness by turning to God. It's what I was sent to do."

One day, Jesus was preaching to a crowd on the beach when He noticed Peter and Andrew, who were fishermen, washing their nets. Jesus jumped into their boat and asked them to take Him a little way offshore. There He sat and spoke to the people from a safe distance.

When Jesus finished preaching, He asked Peter to steer the boat into deeper waters and to lower his nets.

"Master, we fished all night last night and caught nothing," Peter protested. "As it's you who's asking, we'll have another go."

When the brothers tried to pull up their nets, they were so heavy with fish that they could hardly lift them. They had to call to James and John in another boat for help.

When the two boats were nearly sinking under the weight of the catch, Peter knelt at Jesus's feet.

"Lord," Peter said, "I'm not worthy to be one of your followers. I didn't really trust you. I didn't really believe that we'd catch anything."

"Don't be afraid," Jesus said. "From now on, all of you are going to be catching people instead of fish."

The men left behind everything they had and dedicated their lives to following Jesus.

Jesus and the disciples

A disciple is someone who learns from another person and seeks to do what they say and live how they live. There were many disciples of Jesus. He chose 12 of them to do special work for God.

Fishermen

Many people who lived around the Sea of Galilee were fishermen. They fished from boats at night, or waded into the waters in the day to throw nets over the smaller fish in the shallows by the shore, in the same way as the fishermen shown here. The Sea was well stocked with many kinds of edible fish that were sold locally.

Demons

Some people who seemed insane, or mad, were thought to be possessed by demons. People believed demons to be beings who wanted to stop God's work.

Jesus the Healer

PEOPLE far and wide got to hear about Jesus. So many men and women came to see Jesus that the synagogues weren't big enough to fit them all in. With everyone lining up to be healed, Jesus could hardly find a moment to Himself to go off and pray. The authorities began to grumble at how whole towns would grind to a halt when the exciting new preacher arrived. Everyone would down tools and go off to hear Him talk.

Jesus didn't mean to cause trouble. He was just concerned to spread His message to as many folk as possible and help all those who were in need.

In one city, a leper crept up to Jesus one day and knelt at His feet. "Lord, I know that if you want to, you can cure me," the poor man begged, his skin crumbled and deformed with the terrible disease.

"Of course I want to," said Jesus, gently. "Be clean." And Jesus reached out and touched his skin.

The leper was shocked. After all, his deadly disease was so infectious that most people ran off screaming if they saw him coming. Then he realized that Jesus was smiling at him. The leper looked at his fingers. He felt his face. He peered down at his legs. He couldn't believe it! He was cured! His skin was smooth and healthy! Weeping with joy, he thanked Jesus over and over again.

"Don't tell anyone about this," Jesus said. "Go straight to the priest and make an offering of thanks to God."

The overjoyed leper couldn't contain himself. He went leaping about the streets on his brand new legs, waving his healthy arms in the air, telling everyone he met about how the wonderful Jesus had cured him.

So Jesus's reputation spread even further afield and even more people came travelling to see the extraordinary man. Instead of going to towns, Jesus began to preach in the wide open spaces of the countryside, where there was room for everyone.

On another occasion, Jesus was preaching in a private house to a crowd that included many important teachers of the law. Priests, elders and Pharisees had come from towns and cities all over Galilee and Judea, and even from the great city of Jerusalem itself, to question Jesus. They wondered who He really was. A trickster? A prophet with healing powers like Elijah and Elisha? Could He possibly be the Messiah, as so many people were claiming?

> **" Great multitudes gathered to hear and to be healed of their infirmities. "**

As usual, there wasn't even standing room inside the little house. People were crammed together so tightly that they couldn't even raise a hand to scratch their nose. Others spilled out into the passage that led to the street.

While Jesus spoke, four latecomers began struggling to push their way inside. Their job was made even more difficult because they carried a friend of theirs on a stretcher, a man who was paralysed. The ranks of spectators were too dense. There was only one thing for it.

Sweating with the strain, the men carried their friend up the outside stairs on to the flat roof of the house. They tied ropes to the stretcher and removed some of the roof covering. Then, very slowly and carefully, they lowered the stretcher through the gap and down into the room where Jesus was teaching.

Jesus was extremely moved at the friends' faith and at the plight of the paralysed man.

"Take heart, my son," he said, "your sins are forgiven."

All the Pharisees and Saducees present were horrified. It was one thing to have the power of healing, but how could anyone have the power of forgiveness? Only God had that! It was blasphemy!

Jesus soon put a stop to their grumblings.

"I know just as well as you that anyone can say, 'Your sins are forgiven,'" He said. "After all, no one can see whether they really have been or not. To prove to you that God has granted me this power and has healed this man's soul, I shall heal his body too."

Jesus turned again to where the man lay stiff and still on his stretcher.

"Rise up and walk," He commanded.

To everyone's amazement, the man immediately stood up and rolled up his stretcher. Then, praising God, he hurried off to show his family, his grateful friends cheering and slapping him on the back.

The priests, elders and Pharisees didn't dare say a single word more. How could they? What they had just seen was truly astonishing. In fact, everyone agreed they had never seen anything like it before.

JESUS COULD SEE THE MAN HAD A DEEPER NEED THAN JUST TO HAVE HIS BODY HEALED. EVERYONE NEEDS FORGIVENESS FOR THEIR SPIRITUAL 'SICKNESS' – THE SIN THAT KEEPS THEM AWAY FROM GOD.

Pharisees
They were a group of powerful religious leaders who believed that the only way to be right with God was to keep every one of His laws all the time. Pharisees were sincere people, but they hindered others' faith, so Jesus often criticized them.

◆ ABOUT THE STORY ◆

This story shows that Jesus wasn't out to get lots of publicity, His main concern was for the people He helped. Jesus's miracles were not a way of seeking attention, He wanted what was best for people. Jesus knew that people might be attracted to Him by miracles. He also knew, though, that such things would not make them want to trust their lives to God, which was what He wanted.

Matthew is Called

JESUS was walking down a road one day with His many disciples when He looked into an open window and saw a man working at a desk. The man was Levi, later known as Matthew, and he was working in the tax office.

At that time, Judea was under the rule of the Roman empire. The Jews hated everything to do with the conquering nation and its army. They had to pay the Romans in taxes, and the people who collected the taxes for the Romans were seen as traitors. As a result, if you became a tax collector, people you had been friends with for years suddenly stopped talking to you. Even members of your own family didn't want to know you any more. Complete strangers would shout at you in the street, calling you names.

Matthew was one of these hated tax collectors. And while many citizens in the town had taken the day off to see Jesus, Matthew knew he wouldn't be welcome among the crowds of the city. He stayed indoors, busily hunched over his tax records.

Matthew was trying hard to concentrate on his work, when he suddenly felt that someone was watching him. The hair bristled on his neck and he swung round. Matthew found himself looking straight at a stranger who was staring in at

him through the open window – a stranger with the kindest face and deepest, darkest eyes he'd ever seen. Matthew knew it was Jesus.

"Follow me," He said.

Matthew didn't need telling twice. Without a word, he got up out of his chair. He didn't even close his books or put away his pen. He just left everything exactly where it was and hurried off eagerly to join Jesus's disciples.

That night, Matthew insisted that he repay Jesus's kindness by having Him to stay at his house. It was his way of showing how much Jesus meant to him. When

Women disciples
There were also female disciples who were following Jesus. They looked after the practical needs of the twelve. They also listened to and learned from Jesus.

Metal cup
Most ordinary people drank out of pottery cups or out of small bowls. Silver cups like this would be used only by rich people and in the temple.

Tax collectors
Tax collectors were in charge of collecting a wide variety of taxes for the Romans, that they used to pay for their empire.

it. Surely, they thought, Jesus should be sitting down to eat with us, rather than with the common folk? And not just peasants, but tax collectors! Sinners!

The Pharisees grew even more annoyed when Jesus told them off for their moaning.

"Those who are well have no need of a doctor," He explained. "It is those who are ill who need to be healed. I have not been sent to look after good people; it is sinners who have most need of me."

> ❝ *Jesus said to Matthew, 'Follow me.' And he rose and followed Him.* ❞

Jesus had invited him to go along with His followers, Matthew hadn't wanted anyone to notice him. He hadn't jumped up and down for joy, shouting aloud for all to hear. Inside, his heart was dancing. And he was sure that Jesus somehow knew how he felt.

Matthew threw the greatest feast that he could offer Jesus and His disciples. He didn't really have any friends of his own to share the joyous occasion with, so he invited other tax collectors along instead. For the first time ever, Matthew's house was full of guests enjoying themselves – and he loved it.

When the Pharisees got to hear of it, they were very jealous! The Pharisees were devoutly religious and considered themselves better than other people because of

"We try so hard to live good, strict lives!" they protested. "Our followers often fast and pray, as do the disciples of John the Baptist. We never see yours doing the same. Your followers always eat well and drink merrily, as if they're at an eternal banquet! What's it all about?"

"Would you expect guests at a wedding not to celebrate while the bridegroom is present?" Jesus scolded. "There will be plenty of time for fasting when the bridegroom is taken away from the guests."

Jesus's mysterious answer infuriated the Pharisees all the more. Even His disciples didn't really understand. They didn't mind too much. Jesus often seemed to talk in riddles. He always seemed to know more than He was letting on. His followers realized that He explained everything He thought they needed to know. They trusted that the rest would all unfold in its own good time.

The Roman Empire
Jesus lived in Galilee under the rule of the Roman Empire. This was the largest empire in the world at the time. Emperor Augustus brought stability to the Empire and secured the borders.

❖ ABOUT THE STORY ❖

Jesus was known as a friend of tax collectors and people who were regarded as sinners. To have a former tax collector as one of His inner circle of disciples made Him even more odious to the religious leaders, who regarded such people as beyond God's help. Jesus said He came to call all sorts of people to follow God, and this was shown in His choice of disciples.

The Faithful Centurion

Jesus befriended many people who were despised by other Jews. One day, He helped a non-Jewish officer in the Roman army.

It all began when a group of elders came hurrying up to Jesus when He was preaching one day in the town of Capernaum.

"Sir, we have been sent to find you by a Roman centurion," one began.

"He has a loyal servant who he's grown to love like his own son," interrupted another.

"But the servant is very ill," butted in yet another.

"You really should help him out," another elder added. "Even though the centurion is a gentile and an enemy of Israel, he's always been very good to us Jews. He even helped to build our synagogue..."

> *He is worthy to have you do this for him, for he loves our nation, and he built us our synagogue.*

Even before they had finished talking, Jesus was already striding along on His way to the centurion's house.

Jesus had very nearly reached the centurion's house when some people came dashing out of it.

"We have a message for you," they told Jesus. "Our friend says he's not worthy to have you honour his home with your presence, and that is why he never dreamed of coming to see you himself. He begs you not to trouble yourself any further. Instead, he says that if you simply say

Chemists

Although Jesus healed many people, most of the time people had to rely on the medicine of the time. Chemists used herbal remedies for everything, because there were no drugs. Some of these may have been useful, but others were not. Many chemists were con-men, and would just cheat the people.

Jesus often used His miracles to teach something as well. He said people should trust God and accept His word. That is what faith is all about, today as well as then.

Surgical instruments

Compared with modern standards, Roman surgery was very crude, but for the time it was well advanced. The bronze instruments shown here are (from top to bottom) forceps, a spoon, a spatula and a scalpel.

the word of command, his servant will be healed. After all, he's a centurion. He's used to giving orders and finding that everything then happens just so!"

Jesus's face lit up with happiness.

"I tell you, I haven't found such faith among any of you Jews," He told the crowds who were following Him. "There will be people from far-off nations who are allowed to enter the kingdom of heaven, while many from the nation of Israel will be left outside in the darkness, to howl and gnash their teeth in despair."

Jesus turned away and the centurion's friends began to hurry back to the house. They found the servant was completely recovered, just as if he had never been ill.

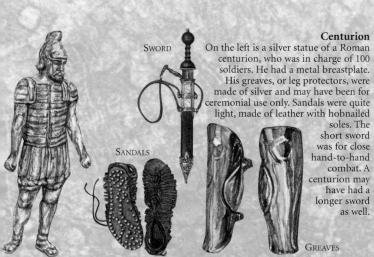

Centurion

SWORD

On the left is a silver statue of a Roman centurion, who was in charge of 100 soldiers. He had a metal breastplate. His greaves, or leg protectors, were made of silver and may have been for ceremonial use only. Sandals were quite light, made of leather with hobnailed soles. The short sword was for close hand-to-hand combat. A centurion may have had a longer sword as well.

SANDALS

GREAVES

✤ ABOUT THE STORY ✤

This story is told to show Jesus's character and His spiritual authority. He only has to say a word, and all creation responds. Here, a man is healed. On a later occasion, a storm was stopped. The Jews knew God had created the world by speaking words of command. There was only one conclusion they could come to. Jesus was God in human form, with all the authority of God.

Trouble Begins to Brew

Day by day, as Jesus's friends grew in number, so did His enemies. Jesus first came up against opposition in Nazareth. You might think that the people of His home town would be proud of the famous local boy. When they heard Him preaching in the synagogue, telling them all kinds of new things they should and shouldn't be doing, they were irritated and envious.

"Where on earth did He get all this wisdom and the knowledge to do all these amazing things?" they scoffed.

"He's only the son of Joseph the carpenter, after all. We know His family: Mary, His mother, and all His brothers and sisters! He's just a normal person like us!"

Jesus was deeply saddened by their lack of belief. There was nothing He could do but turn His back on Nazareth. The people had wasted their chance to hear His message.

Elsewhere, Jesus couldn't help offending other people because His teachings were so new and fresh. The priests and elders, Sadducees and Pharisees, had spent their lives studying the ancient scriptures, but Jesus often presented them in a very different light.

"It's all right to eat all kinds of food," Jesus preached. "It's not what goes into people that is unclean, but what comes out of them, such as evil thoughts, pride, violence. You don't have to stick to all the traditional washing rituals, either. They don't cleanse your soul, as the Pharisees believe they do. They only cleanse your body."

> ❝ *But they were filled with fury and discussed with one another what they might do to Jesus.* ❞

Of course, the holy men who had been doing their best to follow these laws for years, believing they were doing the right thing, were furious to hear Jesus telling them it wasn't necessary. And sometimes He even criticized them openly, saying that they had lost sight of what God's commandments were really all about and that they were just practising meaningless traditions.

What annoyed the Jewish leaders most was the way in which – in their eyes – Jesus broke the laws of the Sabbath. One Sabbath morning, some Pharisees were with Jesus and His disciples walking through a cornfield. Now even though no Jews were allowed to eat until later in the day, Jesus's hungry followers were pulling the heads off the stalks and eating the grain.

"Don't you remember what David once did when he was desperate for food?" Jesus told the angry Pharisees. "He ate the holy bread that only priests are allowed to eat. You should make sure you remember that the Sabbath was made for people, not people for the Sabbath."

Jesus regularly healed people on the holy day. The Jewish elders considered this to be work and therefore a sin. On one occasion, He healed a crippled woman who had been bent double in terrible pain for 18 years.

"None of you would think anything of untying a donkey or ass on the Sabbath to let it drink," Jesus explained, "so shouldn't I set this woman free from her bonds?"

Another time, Jesus healed a man who had a dreadfully deformed and paralysed hand.

"Do you think it's right to do good or evil on the Sabbath?" He challenged the fuming holy men and scribes. "Do you think

that on God's holy day we should save life or destroy it?"

One Sabbath, Jesus went to the pool of Bethesda, where lots of sick and injured people used to gather in the hope of a miraculous cure. It was said that now and again an angel would stir up the water and the first person then to plunge into the pool would be cured. Jesus knew that one crippled man in particular had been waiting by the pool for a long time. For whenever he saw ripples on the water, he couldn't drag himself to the pool fast enough and someone else always beat him there. Jesus was filled with pity and simply said, "Pick up your bed and walk." To the man's delight, he found he could do exactly that. Many of the Jews who saw and heard about the miracle weren't so pleased. They were sure that His healing on the Sabbath was breaking God's commandments. Jesus's answer annoyed them even more. "My Father doesn't stop working on the Sabbath and neither do I," He told them.

"How dare He call God His Father!" the priests and elders gasped, totally outraged. "It's blasphemy!"

Jesus just shrugged.

"It is God my Father who has given me the authority to perform miracles such as these, to raise the dead to life and to judge sinners. I warn you that the day is coming soon when everyone will hear the voice of the Son of God calling them to be judged – even the dead will come forth to be either rewarded or punished."

The Jewish leaders were fuming, but Jesus carried on.

"You search the scriptures to find out how to win eternal life. Even though Moses wrote that I would be coming, you refuse to follow me. If you don't believe Moses, how do you expect to believe what I am telling you?"

So it was that many of the priests and elders, Pharisees and Sadducees, became Jesus's enemies. Little by little, more and more of them began to gather together in secret to plot ways in which they might get rid of Him...

Pool of Bethesda
Bethesda was like a health spa. The pool is probably one of two which can be seen near St Anne's Church in Jerusalem today. Legend said that the first person to enter the pool after it was touched by an angel would be healed.

J ESUS DID NOT BREAK GOD'S LAW, BUT HE DID BREAK THE RULES PEOPLE HAD ADDED TO GOD'S. HIS ACTION REMINDS PEOPLE TO CHECK THAT THEIR TRADITIONS DON'T STOP PEOPLE KNOWING GOD. 〜

❖ **ABOUT THE STORY** ❖

The Sabbath (the seventh day of the week, our Saturday) is special for the Jews. God was said to have rested from creation on the seventh day. People were commanded to rest and remember God on that day. Jesus was later raised from the dead on Sunday, the first day of the week, and for Christians Sunday has become their "Sabbath". Jesus said the day was for everyone's benefit.

The Apostles are Appointed

THERE came a time when Jesus said He needed to be alone for a while. Everywhere He went, people clamoured to see Him. So eventually Jesus went on His own up a mountain to pray. All night long the disciples waited for Him to return. At last they saw the familiar figure of Jesus striding towards them.

Jesus called out 12 names: the brothers Peter and Andrew, James and John, Matthew the tax collector, Philip, Bartholomew, James, Thaddaeus, Thomas, Simon the Zealot, and Judas Iscariot. Then He took the puzzled men away from the rest of the disciples, where He could speak to them in private.

"I have something very important to ask of you," Jesus said, seriously. "I need you to help me carry out my mission. I want you to split up and go off on your own into the countryside. Preach my message as you go. Tell all the people that the kingdom of heaven will soon be here. I am going to give each of you special powers. I want you to heal the sick as I do, to raise people from the dead for me, to cleanse lepers and to cast out demons from those who are possessed by evil."

The 12 men looked at each other anxiously.

"Furthermore, I want you to do all this for nothing," Jesus continued. "You mustn't take any payment from anyone. I don't want you to take anything with you – not even a bag with a

---

THE APOSTLES HAD TO RELY ON GOD FOR EVERYTHING. TODAY, WE TEND TO ASK GOD ONLY FOR WHAT WE CAN'T GET OURSELVES. THIS STORY ENCOURAGES US TO RELY ON GOD AND NOT TO WORRY.

The 12 apostles
This mosaic from Italy is one artist's attempt to show what the 12 apostles looked like. The word apostle means "one who is sent". With the exception of Judas Iscariot, they all became leaders of the Christian Church after Jesus died.

change of clothing or a spare pair of sandals. You must rely on finding good people in the towns you visit who will put you up and look after you."

The friends all nodded, listening very carefully.

"It will not be an easy job," Jesus went on. "You have already seen the problems I face. If anyone refuses to listen, don't get dismayed. Just go on your way and shake off your disappointment, just as you shake the dust from your shoes. However, be wary all the time. I know that I'm sending you out like sheep heading straight for a pack of wolves. There will be people who will hear you and follow you, but there will be others who make up their minds to hate you because you are my representative. They will try and arrest you, and they'll haul you before royal courts to order you to stop spreading my message. Don't be afraid. At times like these, the Holy Spirit will give you courage and tell you what to say. You shouldn't fear people, because they can hurt only your body, not your soul. Have great fear of the Lord, for He can destroy both your body and soul in the fires of hell. My Father in heaven will be looking after you all the way."

> *And they departed and went through the villages, healing everywhere.*

Jesus was pleased to see that the 12 men He had chosen looked determined.

"Don't think that I have come to bring peace on earth," He told them. "I have come to bring a sword that will carve up the righteous from the wicked. Anyone who does not take up his cross and follow me, bearing the responsibilities that go with this, will not find heaven. If you give up your lives to me – even perhaps dying for my sake – you will be given new lives."

From that day onwards, the 12 men were known as the apostles. And for several weeks, they went out on their own around the countryside, teaching and healing. And when they returned, they were full of the wondrous miracles they had been able to perform in Jesus's name.

❖ ABOUT THE STORY ❖

Jesus spent much of His time with the 12. He gave them more teaching than the rest of the disciples, and He trained and equipped them to take over His mission when He died. Despite all their experience with Jesus, they still didn't fully understand His mission until after His resurrection. Then it became clear, and they were ready for their special work.

The Sermon on the Mount

ONE day, Jesus went up a mountain so everyone could hear Him.

"Blessed are all those people who realize that God is missing from their lives, for heaven will be theirs. Blessed are those who are full of sorrow, for they will be comforted. Blessed are the gentle, for they will be given the earth. Blessed are those who hunger and thirst for goodness, for they will receive what they desire. Blessed are those who are merciful, for they will have mercy shown to them, too. Blessed are those with pure, true hearts, for they will see God. Blessed are those who strive for peace; God considers them His own children.

> **" If anyone strikes you on the right cheek, turn to him the other also. "**

Blessed are all those who are made to suffer because they are trying to do right, for theirs is the kingdom of heaven. If others mock you and make your life miserable because you follow my teachings, you should rejoice and be glad, for you will win a wonderful reward in heaven! You are the light of the world, so shine like beacons to lead others to God."

The crowds were amazed at Jesus's words.

"Don't think that I'm telling you to forget the law or abandon the teachings of the prophets," Jesus continued. "I'm not. You need to pay more attention to them than ever. The law says that you should not kill anyone; I'm

Church of the Mount of Beatitudes
This church is built where Jesus is believed to have preached the Sermon on the Mount. The sayings that begin with the word "Blessed" at the beginning of the sermon are known as Beatitudes.

The Lord's Prayer
Jesus gave this prayer as a model, rather than simply a prayer to be recited. In it are all the main elements of prayer. It addresses God as Father, who can be trusted to provide all we need. It worships Him and puts His will first. It seeks forgiveness and thinks well of others. It asks for God's protection, as well as for His provision of our basic needs.

THE LORD'S PRAYER

OUR FATHER WHO ART IN HEAVEN,
HALLOWED BE THY NAME.
THY KINGDOM COME,
THY WILL BE DONE,
ON EARTH AS IT IS IN HEAVEN.
GIVE US THIS DAY OUR DAILY BREAD;
AND FORGIVE US OUR TRESPASSES,
AS WE FORGIVE THOSE WHO
TRESPASS AGAINST US;
AND LEAD US NOT INTO TEMPTATION,
BUT DELIVER US FROM EVIL.
FOR THINE IS THE KINGDOM, THE POWER
AND THE GLORY, FOR EVER AND EVER.
AMEN.

telling you that you shouldn't even argue with anyone. The law says that you shouldn't go off with another person's husband or wife; I'm telling you that you shouldn't even think about it. If what you can see is leading you to sin, then gouge out your eyes. It's better to lose part of your body than have your whole body burnt in the fires of hell because you have sinned. The law says that you are entitled to take revenge on someone who wrongs you. I'm telling you that you should do nothing to get your own back. In fact, if someone hits your right cheek, turn the left towards them so they can strike that too. The law says love your neighbours and hate your enemies. I'm telling you to love your enemies, too. You should be kind and generous to all people, no matter who they are."

The crowds looked up at the preacher in awe.

"Now," Jesus went on, "many people like everyone to know that they give money to the needy and they go every day to the synagogue, making sure that everyone knows about it. God will not reward these people in heaven, for they have already received the admiration of those on earth. Don't show off your good works and boast about them. Do your fasting and giving to charity in secret, not so everyone knows, and when you pray, use these simple words..."

And Jesus taught the crowds to pray.

"Also, don't bother with wealth. The riches of this world can easily be stolen or turned to rust. Instead, build up the treasure of good thoughts and deeds that thieves can't get and that won't decay. And don't worry about what you're going to eat or wear. If you put your efforts into searching for God, He'll make sure that you're looked after."

Jesus stretched His arms out to the hundreds of people who were patiently listening, entranced.

Everyone who follows these words of mine will be like a wise man who builds his house on rock, so it stands firm. Anyone who hears what I say and yet takes no notice will be like a fool who builds his house on sand. The winds will blow it down and the rains will wash it away."

Solid foundation
Jesus wanted to make sure that people knew that those who built their "house", or life, on the foundation of faith in God, will be safe and secure.

Andrew and James
Andrew had been a disciple of John the Baptist before he became one of the apostles. James is believed to be the brother of John. They, together with Peter and Andrew, seem to have been fishing partners.

❖ **ABOUT THE STORY** ❖

The Sermon on the Mount was probably not given just in one go. Jesus repeated this teaching on different occasions throughout His ministry. He needed to as it was very different to what people had been taught then. It is still different to what most people do today. It says that God's kingdom is far more valuable than all the riches in the world.

The Parables of the Kingdom

IN His preaching, Jesus told many stories, or parables, to the people.

"Imagine a person walking down a field, scattering grain onto the earth," He said one day. "Some of the seeds will land on the footpath and won't sink into the soil. The birds will swoop down straight away and peck them up. Some of the seeds will fall on to rocky, stony ground. They'll start growing very quickly, but as soon as the sun comes out, they'll be scorched and wither away, because they don't have any deep roots. Other seeds will fall into thorny patches of weeds. The brambles and briars will grow faster than the corn and choke it. The seeds that fall on to good soil will grow up tall and strong into a plentiful crop."

The listening crowds looked up anxiously at Jesus, waiting for Him to explain what it all meant.

Jesus just said, "Now everyone go away and work out what the story means."

Later in the day, when the disciples were alone with Jesus, they questioned Him about how He had handled the crowds.

"Jesus, why do you tell the people parables and then leave them to try to understand for themselves?" the disciples asked. "When you're with the 12 of us in private, you always explain everything."

Jesus sighed. "You have been given the gift to understand all the secrets I tell you about the kingdom of heaven," He explained. "Other people, who haven't been privileged in this way, wouldn't understand. So I teach them through stories. This way, the more carefully they listen and the harder they try to understand, the more they will get out of them and the closer they will get to the kingdom of heaven. For many of them look at me, but they don't really see who I am. They listen to me, but they don't really hear what I'm saying. They think they're taking in my words, but they don't really understand."

And He explained to the disciples what the parable of the sower meant.

> **And He told them many things in parables.**

"The seed is the word of God. The footpath stands for those who hear the word of God but who don't take it in. The devil will swoop down straight away and steal the message away from them. The rocky ground represents those who pay attention to the word of God and take it on board for a short while. Because the message hasn't sunk deep enough into their hearts, any difficulties that arise will overcome them and they will give up on it. The weeds

are those who hear the word of God but who are either too worried about their daily problems, or simply too busy having a good time, to do anything about it. The good soil stands for those who absorb the word of God deep within themselves. They give it a place to grow, and over time they bear good fruit."

Jesus explained other parables to the disciples. He told a story about a sower, whose enemy had secretly planted weeds among his crops. When the sower's servants saw the shoots appear, they asked him if he wanted them to go and pull them out. The sower was worried that they'd get confused and pull the good plants out with the bad ones. "Leave it till harvest time," he told them. "Then I'll tell my reapers to pull out the weeds first and burn them, leaving the corn to be safely gathered in." Jesus explained that the sower was the Son of God and the field was the world. The seeds were people who loved God and the weeds people who opposed God. He said that at the end of time, the Son of God would send His angels to cast the bad people into hell, leaving the good people to live happily in the kingdom of heaven.

Once, Jesus compared the kingdom of heaven to a grain of mustard. "It is a small seed," He said, "but it will grow into a massive bush and birds will nest in its branches."

Other parables showed how determined people had to be to enter the kingdom. They needed to be like a pearl merchant who sees the most precious pearl of all and sells everything he has in order to buy it. Or a person who discovers buried treasure in a field. He covers it up again, and he rushes away to sell everything that he owns, just so that he can buy the field. God's kingdom is like the treasure, you must want it more than anything else.

Jesus warned everyone to listen hard to the stories He told. "No one goes out to buy a lamp and then covers it up or puts it under the bed, so its light is hidden," He said. "So having come to hear me, make sure you don't ignore my teachings. For what I am telling you, everyone will one day know to be the truth."

Sower's bag
Farmers sowed their seed by hand. They ploughed the soil then walked up and down throwing handfuls of seed from the bag slung over their shoulder. Usually, they then ploughed the field again, or drove animals over it, to push the seed into the soil.

Grain sieve
Grain was always sifted in a shallow basket like this before being ground to make flour for bread. Some weed seeds might be mixed in with it which would poison the bread. Some weed seeds were picked out by hand and the contents of the basket shaken so that any remaining seeds which were smaller than the grain, would drop out of the holes.

❧ ABOUT THE STORY ❧

These parables built up a picture of what the kingdom of God was like. It isn't something that could be illustrated in one simple picture. Together the parables show that it is God's rules working in people's lives. Therefore the kingdom of God can be anywhere. It grows as more people learn to serve God and influence others for good. It is worth more than anything else because it lasts for ever.

Jesus Stills the Storm

JESUS was exhausted. He'd been preaching all day by the Sea of Galilee to crowds that were bigger than ever. His throat was hoarse and His legs and back were aching. He'd already tried to tell the people that He'd finished for the day.

Even though it was now growing dark, it was obvious that many didn't want to go home. They were still lurking about in groups, waiting to see where Jesus was going next, so they could follow Him.

"Let's sail over to the other side of the lake," Jesus said to His disciples. "We might be able to be on our own there for a while."

They splashed along the seashore to their boat and pushed off, raising the little sail. As the boat cut through the waters, Jesus sank into a deep sleep down at the back of the boat, rocked by the rise and fall of the waves and lulled by the swish of the sea.

While Jesus dreamed, the disciples were horrified to notice dark clouds racing across the sky and heading straight for them. Before they'd even had time to furl the sail, the wind began to whip up around them. It wailed and howled, stirring up the waters into great peaks that tossed the little boat into the air and then plunged them down towards the depths.

> " *Why are you afraid, O men of little faith?* "

Of course, Peter, Andrew, James and John were used to storms like this. They were fishermen and had often been caught in them.

"Don't worry," Peter called out cheerfully, "it's just a little breeze. Nothing to be sick about!"

He showed them how to tie the sails down, and how to bale out the water which splashed over the side and made their feet cold.

However, it wasn't just a little breeze. It was the most horrendous storm they had ever known. It was as if a giant hand was shaking the boat, trying to make it sink.

"I'm scared!" shouted one of the disciples.

"I can't swim!" cried another.

Soon, even Peter was terrified. Some clung on to the sides of the boat and the mast for dear life, drenched by the waves that came crashing on to the deck, threatening to wash them overboard. Others were thrown to and fro as they rushed back and forth, trying desperately to bale out the water that swamped the boat. Through it all, Jesus went on sleeping undisturbed.

"Master! Master!" the terrified disciples cried, their voices nearly drowned out by the screaming of the gale. "Wake up! We're all going to drown!"

Jesus opened one sleepy eyelid and sat up, sleepily. He yawned and stretched, then stood up in the front of the boat to face the full force of the storm.

"Peace!" He thundered, reaching His arms up towards the black, raging skies.

"Be still!" He bellowed, stretching His hands out over the billowing waters.

At once the howling died away, the wind dropped and the sail hung limply in the still air. The sea suddenly flattened into a glassy mirror, its surface barely disturbed by a single ripple. The clouds were blown from the evening skies, until a still, starry night hung over the peaceful little boat.

Jesus turned to face the trembling disciples.

"Why were you afraid?" He asked the astounded men, as they cowered away from Him in complete awe. "You have such little faith."

Then He lay down once more and drifted off to sleep, just as if the danger had never happened.

As the disciples stirred themselves from their shock and turned the boat back on track for the far shore, they couldn't stop whispering about what they had witnessed.

THE DISCIPLES FORGOT ONE IMPORTANT FACT: GOD WOULD NOT LET HIS SON PERISH IN AN ACCIDENT BEFORE HIS WORK WAS COMPLETED. INSTEAD OF PANICKING, THEY SHOULD HAVE TRUSTED GOD.

Storm on Sea of Galilee
The Sea of Galilee is surrounded by steep hills. During the afternoon, the hot air which rises off the lake cools over the hills and can form storm clouds. This then rushes down the steep hills and whips up the lake into a boiling cauldron.

☙ ABOUT THE STORY ❧

Jesus teaches two things through this extraordinary storm. One is that He trusted the disciples to look after the boat, which is why He was asleep. The second is that He showed Himself to be Lord of creation. He has complete power over natural forces. The message is that with Jesus "on board" a person's life, there is nothing to fear.

Legion and the Swine

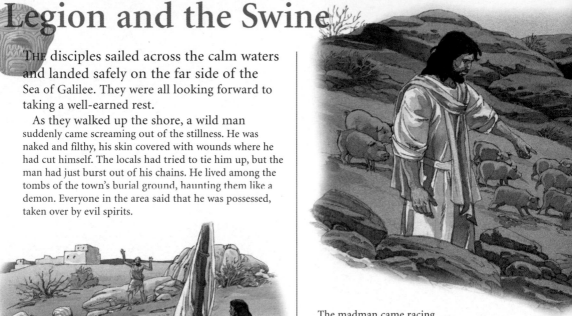

THE disciples sailed across the calm waters and landed safely on the far side of the Sea of Galilee. They were all looking forward to taking a well-earned rest.

As they walked up the shore, a wild man suddenly came screaming out of the stillness. He was naked and filthy, his skin covered with wounds where he had cut himself. The locals had tried to tie him up, but the man had just burst out of his chains. He lived among the tombs of the town's burial ground, haunting them like a demon. Everyone in the area said that he was possessed, taken over by evil spirits.

The madman came racing towards Jesus and flung himself at His feet. He seemed to know His name.

"Jesus, Son of the Most High God, what do you want with me?" the madman slobbered.

Jesus knew that it wasn't the man himself who was really speaking; it was the demons inside him.

"What is your name?" Jesus demanded.

"Legion," the demons inside the madman replied. "For there are whole legions of us inside of him."

Jesus began to tell the evil spirits to get out of the man

Demon possession
People at the time believed that sometimes evil spirits took over a person's life. Examples have been seen in many cultures. Casting out demons is known as exorcism. This is a sculpture of a demon leaving someone's mouth.

Burial ground
Most cultures respect their dead. This is a Middle Eastern burial ground. The one Legion lived in was probably a network of underground caves.

put on clothes, and was sitting calmly by Jesus's side. The townspeople couldn't understand what had happened. Who was this stranger to command evil spirits like that?

> **"** *The whole herd rushed down the steep bank into the sea, and perished in the waters.* **"**

"Keep away from us!" the nervous locals yelled. Jesus sighed and picked Himself up and went back to the boat.

Legion ran after them. "I can't thank you enough! Please, take me with you," the grateful man begged.

Jesus took his hand. "Go back to the home you once had," He said. "I want you to tell everyone how much God has done for you."

and leave him alone. "Don't send us into hell!" shrieked the demons. "Let us live somewhere else, such as in those pigs."

Jesus looked at the snuffling animals nearby.

"Go!" He commanded the demons.

At once, the pigs began to grunt in terror. Then they galloped wildly down the slopes to the cliff edge and dived to their deaths on the rocks below.

The petrified herdsmen fled in terror. Soon they were back with anxious townspeople. Legion had washed and

Monastery at Kursi
The exact site where this story took place is unknown, but this Byzantine monastery at Kursi was built where tradition said Legion had been cured.

Demon mask
This terracotta mask comes from Babylon. It shows the giant Humbaba. Masks like this were the Babylonians' way of trying to keep the demons away.

❧ ABOUT THE STORY ❧

Pigs were unclean animals to the Jews. The demons going into a herd of pigs was a clear sign that the spirits were unclean, or evil. It was perhaps also a rebuke to the people for not living their lives according to the laws of God. The reaction of the townspeople was one of guilt. God's presence among them was unsettling. They preferred the devil they knew to the God they didn't.

Healed by Faith

One day, a synagogue leader called Jairus pushed his way through the hundreds of people surrounding Jesus and knelt down at the surprised preacher's feet.

"Master," he pleaded, ignoring those jostling him from all sides. "My little daughter is only 12 years old and she is dying." He looked up at Jesus with a tear-stained face. "I beg you to come and lay your hands on her to make her well again."

Jesus immediately stood up and set off after Jairus. And as usual, the massive crowd went with Him, surrounding Him on all sides, pulling and elbowing each other out of the way to be as close as possible to the great teacher.

They hadn't gone very far when, without any warning, Jesus suddenly stopped and span round. The startled crowd fell silent.

"Who touched me?" He said, scanning the rows of anxious faces. "Who reached out and touched my robe?"

The people hung their heads and waited for the person to step forward.

"Master," said Peter quietly, "there are people pressing in on you from all sides. You are struggling to walk along because everyone's pushing you back and forth. How can you ask who has touched you?"

"Somebody in particular reached out for me," Jesus

explained. "I felt power go out of me."

Jesus's eyes singled out a woman in the crowd.

"Don't be afraid," He said. "Come here." And the people fell back to let the trembling lady through.

> ❝ The girl is not dead, but sleeping. ❞

The woman had been ill for 12 years with a painful disease. She had been to many doctors in the hope of a cure, but if anything, they had made her worse. Yet she had had great faith in Jesus. She had truly believed that He had the power to cure her. Even if she couldn't get to see Him or speak to Him, she had been determined to get close enough to touch Him, for that, she had felt, would be enough. As the crowds had pushed and shoved round Jesus as He walked along, the woman had seized her chance. She had pressed her way forwards as near to Jesus as she could, then thrust her arm out between the people in front of her. Her fingers had just scraped the edge of Jesus's robe.

"My daughter," Jesus said to the woman, gently. "It is your faith that has made you well."

All this time, Jairus was waiting anxiously. Please hurry up, he was thinking, or it will be too late. Just as Jesus was finishing speaking to the woman, Jairus saw one of his

servants approaching. His heart sank.

"My lord," the servant said gently. "Don't trouble the preacher any further. I'm afraid that your daughter is dead."

Jesus had overheard. He put His hand on the heartbroken Jairus's arm.

"Don't worry," He said. "Trust me. She'll be all right."

When Jesus, Jairus and the crowd of followers reached Jairus's house, the mourners were already there, weeping and wailing outside.

"Don't be so upset," Jesus told them. "The girl isn't dead at all. She's just in a deep sleep."

The mourners scoffed at His kind words. Some of them even laughed. Jesus took no notice. Taking only Jairus and his wife, and His three friends Peter, John and James, He made His way to the room where the body lay, stiff and cold. Tenderly, Jesus held the little girl's hand.

"My child," He whispered, "it's time to get up now."

The girl opened her eyes wide and sat up on the bed.

Even though Jesus told the overjoyed parents not to tell anyone what he had done, it wasn't long before news of the miracle was all over the countryside.

Jesus and hope
This mosaic shows Jesus wearing a blue robe. The artist showed Jesus wearing blue because it is the colour of hope. This is because it resembles the sky. It was this faith and hope that Jesus liked and admired, and wanted people to have.

❧ ABOUT THE STORY ❧

The first woman demonstrated her true faith in Jesus. She knew that if she touched Him she would be cured. But she delayed Jesus so much that Jairus's daughter was dead before Jesus got to her. Many people would say that Jesus got His priorities wrong. By doing what He did, Jesus meets the needs of young and old equally.

The Death of John the Baptist

JOHN the Baptist was thrown into prison by King Herod Antipas of Judea because he had criticized the king's marriage to his niece Herodias. The marriage broke the law of Moses because the couple were related, and they had both had to divorce their partners in order to marry.

John was all alone in prison and his mind was troubled. He sent his followers to ask Jesus if He really was the one the world was waiting for.

"Tell John everything you have seen," Jesus told John's disciples. "The blind see, the lame walk, lepers are healed, the deaf can hear, the poor are cheered in spirit, and the dead are raised to life."

He paid tribute to the great preacher.

"John the Baptist is the greatest person ever born," He told them, "but many people have refused to listen to him, just as they now fail to listen to me."

King Herod's new wife had tried to make King Herod execute John. Herod did not dare kill such a righteous man, no matter what he had said.

One day, the king threw a massive banquet and his daughter, Salome, danced for him.

Herod clapped his hands in delight.

"That was wonderful," he gushed. "What can I get you to say thank you? Anything you want. You just name it."

Greek dancers
Dancing was a favourite pursuit at ancient banquets. Salome's dance followed in a long tradition that went back hundreds of years. This is a painting from a vase of Greek dancers, from 500BC. Salome's dance has often been portrayed in music and dance since. A composer called Richard Strauss wrote a whole opera called *Salome*.

Symbol of Rome
The eagle, seen here on a round base, was the symbol of the Roman Empire.

Wedding statue
This Roman relief shows the bride and groom holding hands while a third person reads out the legal contract.

The best the king could do was to return John's body to his followers. His horrified disciples buried him and then told Jesus the news.

> " *Herodias had a grudge against him, and wanted to kill him.* "

Herod couldn't forget what he had done. And when news came to him of a strange preacher who healed the sick and raised the dead to life, Herod trembled. He thought that perhaps Jesus was John the Baptist risen from the dead.

"Anything?" asked Salome, her eyes opening wide. She dashed off to tell her mother.

"Mother says that I should ask you for the head of John the Baptist," Salome murmured, when she called back.

Herod gasped. He'd made a promise in front of all his guests. He'd have to keep his word, and he ordered John executed. Later that day, Salome took her cruel mother the head of John the Baptist on a plate.

HEROD PAID THE PRICE FOR HIS OWN FOLLY. HE SHOULD NEVER HAVE PROMISED SALOME 'ANYTHING'. MAKING RASH PROMISES IS RARELY A GOOD IDEA. THINGS CAN HAPPEN TO MAKE US REGRET THEM. ∾

The harp
The harp was a popular instrument throughout biblical times and would have been played at Herod's banquet. However, the instrument used in biblical times was more properly called a lyre, because it had fewer strings than a harp.

❖ ABOUT THE STORY ❖

The coming of John the Baptist was foretold in the Scriptures. People were looking for Elijah as the scriptures had said, but Elijah was reborn as John. The fate that John meets foreshadows the death of Jesus Himself. John is executed because of the silly dislikes and jealousy of one person. Jesus is a victim of the jealousy and dislike of a whole group of people.

Jesus's Time and Place

LIFE in Judea at the time when Jesus lived was dominated by the occupying Roman army. Soldiers were everywhere, patrolling the streets to keep law and order as there was no police force.

The soldiers had wide powers. They could order people to do anything for them. Ordinary people could be told to feed soldiers or give them somewhere to sleep. If soldiers were marching somewhere, they could force people to carry their bags or just walk in to their homes and take an ox-cart or pack animal.

The Romans had an efficient system of government. Ruling over the whole empire was the emperor (called Caesar in the Gospels, which was a title rather than a name). Jesus was born during the reign of the great Emperor Augustus, who organized the empire with great efficiency. The emperor during Jesus's ministry was Tiberius. He was a bad emperor. He hardly ever went to Rome and lived a life of indulgent luxury and splendour.

Each province and district had a senior Roman official in charge, usually appointed directly by the emperor. Two such governors are mentioned in the Gospels. Quirinius was in charge of the province of Syria, and Pontius Pilate, who was prefect of Judea and who sentenced Jesus to death by crucifixion. From records outside the gospels we know that Pilate was a cruel man.

The Romans allowed the Jews some freedom, and to have kings in various parts of Judea. All of these were members of the Herod family. Herod the Great had started to build the temple in Jerusalem for the Jews. He died about the time Jesus was born, and his area was split between three of his sons, all of whom are named in the gospels: Herod Philip, Archelaus and Herod Antipas. They had limited, but real, powers to govern aspects of life.

The Roman occupiers were hated. The Herods, though, were thought to have more sympathy with the Romans than with their countrymen, and they were too powerful to displease. The people who collected taxes for the Romans from merchants and ordinary householders, however, were despised and seen as traitors.

The greatest critics of tax collectors were the Pharisees, a group of about 6,000 men. They were very traditional in their beliefs and practices. Jesus often came into conflict with them because they taught that the only way to be right with God was to practise all the tiny laws which they said were contained in the scriptures. The Pharisees were very fussy. Jesus said that they had lost sight of the real meaning of the law. They were so busy sticking to all the tiny little laws that they ignored all the big ones.

Sometimes allied with them were the Sadducees who were a snobbish group of leaders, mostly priests, who only accepted the written laws of the scriptures, not the others

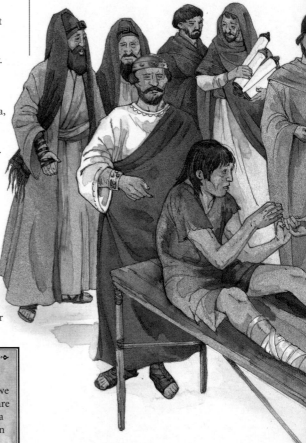

❧ PEOPLE AT THE TIME OF JESUS ❧

This picture shows Jesus healing a paralysed person (centre). Watching him are a number of people who we encounter in the gospels. From left at the back there are two Pharisees and two Sadducees. In the blue robe is a tax collector. Roman soldiers stand at the back, and on the far right are two Essenes. In the foreground is a local governor (left), such as Herod Antipas, and a Roman emperor (right).

which the Pharisees had added. Unlike the Pharisees at the time, they did not believe in life after death.

Other religious groups existed in the area but are not mentioned directly in the gospels. Among them were the Essenes. They were scattered in monastic communities all over Judea, but their most famous community was at Qumran near the Dead Sea, where the Dead Sea scrolls were found. They had a strict rule of life. It is sometimes thought that John the Baptist grew up among the Essenes but there is no direct proof of this.

Dead Sea scrolls

The "Shrine of the Book" is in a museum in Jerusalem where some of the Dead Sea scrolls are kept. They were found in 1947 in caves near Qumran by the Dead Sea and were the library of the community that once lived there. The scrolls contain ancient copies of all the Old Testament books except the Book of Esther.

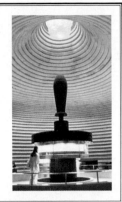

Roman Worship

This is the Temple of Castor and Pollux, the twin gods who the Romans believed helped them win battles. The Romans worshipped many gods, and built temples to them through the Empire.

Gladiators in Rome

The Roman Emperors were famous for putting on grand shows for the Roman citizens. This is the Colosseum, where the Romans made men, called gladiators, fight wild animals and each other.

The Apostles

Jesus had many disciples. The word means "one who learns". They were people who followed Jesus about the countryside whenever they could. They thought about His teaching, watched His actions, and tried to live in the way He taught. At some point early in His ministry, Jesus selected 12 particular disciples to become an inner core, that He would teach to become leaders in the church.

Later, they were called apostles, which means "one who is sent". They were Jesus's agents sent into the world to spread His teaching. At least some of them, such as Peter and Matthew, had been called as individuals first. Jesus taught the apostles privately, and restricted some of His more significant miracles (such as the stilling of the storm) to them alone.

Within the circle of twelve, there was an even smaller inner circle of three: Peter, James and John. We do not know much about the backgrounds of the disciples, but certain things do stand out.

Peter's birth name was Simon, which means "stone" in Greek. He was dubbed Peter (the rock) by Jesus. He was the spokesman of the group. Peter often opened his mouth before thinking, and as a result sometimes offended people. Passionate, impulsive and dedicated, he seems to have been the sort of person who would be your friend for life if he liked you.

He was a fisherman from Lake Galilee, and owned a boat which Jesus used

PETER

from time to time for transport and also as a floating pulpit when he preached to large crowds by the lakeside. At the crucifixion, Peter denied ever knowing Jesus. Filled with remorse he was forgiven, and became the leader of the first Christians. He also became the first disciple to take the gospel to non-Jews. He was martyred in Rome by the emperor Nero about AD66. It is believed that he was the source of information behind Mark's gospel.

The brothers James and John were also fishermen on Galilee and may have beenpartners with Peter and his brother Andrew. James and John were nicknamed "Sons of Thunder" by Jesus. On one famous occasion, they were angry at being rejected by a village. They asked if, by using their new spiritual powers, they should call down some judgement on the people there. Jesus took this opportunity to teach them more about the gentle ways of God.

John, it is believed, wrote the fourth Gospel, the *Book of Revelation*, and the three New Testament letters attributed to him. After Jesus's death he was an elder in the church in Ephesus in Turkey. He was later exiled to the prison island of Patmos in the Aegean.

JOHN

ANDREW

JAMES

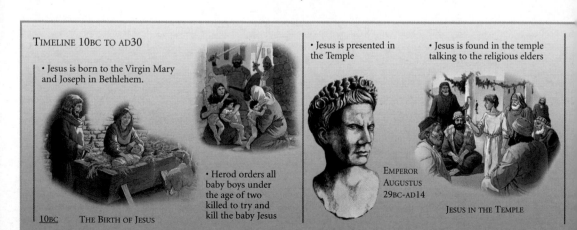

TIMELINE 10BC TO AD30

• Jesus is born to the Virgin Mary and Joseph in Bethlehem.

• Herod orders all baby boys under the age of two killed to try and kill the baby Jesus

• Jesus is presented in the Temple

EMPEROR AUGUSTUS 29BC-AD14

• Jesus is found in the temple talking to the religious elders

10BC   THE BIRTH OF JESUS

JESUS IN THE TEMPLE

James was to become one of the first Christian martyrs, executed by King Herod in about AD43. He is not the same James as the one who later led the church in Jerusalem and wrote the New Testament letter bearing his name.

Andrew, Peter's brother, was not one of the inner circle, but deserves a special mention. He comes across as the most gentle and caring of the disciples. It was Andrew who first brought Peter to Jesus. "Come and see!" he'd cried excitedly to his (probably elder) brother. It was Andrew who saw the possibility of using the five loaves and two fish to feed the 5,000. And it was Andrew who, with Philip, brought some non-Jews to Jesus, too. He was a man of vision. It is believed that he was crucified in Asia Minor in about AD60.

Matthew was a tax collector, also called Levi, and he gave up his despised job to become a disciple. He did not, however, become the treasurer of the group. That job fell to Judas Iscariot, who became infamous later as the one who handed Jesus over to the rulers. Why he did this has remained a mystery. The Gospels indicate he was prompted by the devil. We know that when he saw that Jesus was to be executed, he gave back the money he had been paid to betray him and committed suicide.

Thomas, known as the doubter, was missing from the group when Jesus first appeared to them after the resurrection. He refused to believe their stories. Only later, when he was able to see and touch Jesus for himself, did he believe in His resurrection. The experience was life-changing; it is believed that he went on to form the church in India.

Little is known of the others. There is even some confusion over their names in the gospels (like Peter, many of them seem to have had more than one name). They were Bartholomew, another James, another Simon (also called "the Zealot"), Thaddeus (also called Judas) and Philip.

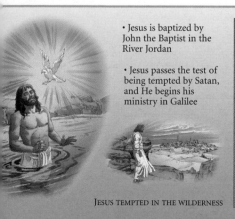

JUDAS

PHILIP

MATTHEW

THADDEUS

THOMAS

BARTHOLOMEW

SIMON

JAMES

• Jesus is baptized by John the Baptist in the River Jordan

• Jesus passes the test of being tempted by Satan, and He begins his ministry in Galilee

JESUS TEMPTED IN THE WILDERNESS

• Jesus performs His first miracle, turning water into wine at the wedding in Cana

THE FIRST MIRACLE

JOHN THE BAPTIST EXECUTED

• John the Baptist is executed by Herod on the request of his daughter, Salome

AD30

Glossary

apostle
The group of twelve men that Jesus picked from His disciples were called apostles. They were the closest people to Him, and learned the most from Him. The group of apostles also includes Saul, who converted to Christianity after Jesus's death.

baptism
Jesus commanded that His followers be baptized to show they had been converted. Baptism involves immersing people in water. John the Baptist baptized many people as a sign of repentance and inner cleansing. The apostle Paul later said that Christian baptism is symbolic. When the person disappears beneath the water and then reappears, they are symbolically undergoing death, burial and resurrection, as Christ did.

disciples
As Jesus travelled round Galilee, teaching and preaching to the people there, people started to follow Him and His way of living. These people were called disciples. From the larger group of the disciples, Jesus chose his particularly close group of followers, called the apostles.

gentile
This is a general terms for nations, and which came to mean anyone who is not Jewish. Jesus made sure that he preached His message to gentiles as well as Jews.

Gospel
Some of the people who followed Jesus's teaching recorded His life and works in writing. These are known as the Gospels, which means "good news". These writings have been passed down through the years and now form part of the New Testament. The Gospels are credited to Matthew, Mark, Luke and John.

kingdom of God
The kingdom of God is not an earthly kingdom. Jesus said that the kingdom of God is within everyone who follows His teachings, and tries to live their life in a Christian way.

Messiah
This means anointed one in Hebrew, the word Christ is the equivalent word in Greek. It means one chosen by God. By the time of Jesus, all the Jews were hoping for a great Messiah-king to set up an everlasting kingdom. Jesus's kingdom, the kingdom of God, was not an earthly kingdom. Jesus was not an emperor commanding armies as many were expecting. The kingdom of God will last forever.

ministry
Jesus spent about three years travelling around Judea, teaching the people about how they should live their lives and respect God. This is called His ministry.

miracle
Jesus performed many miracles during his ministry in Galilee, healing the sick and dying, casting out demons, and even bringing people back from the dead. Miracles are sometimes described as "mighty works", and they are performed through the power of God.

parable
Jesus told stories to people, called parables, to teach them about the kingdom of God. The stories used people and situations that his audience would be familiar with, which made the point of Jesus's story easier for people to remember and to understand.

Pharisee
A strict religious sect, the name Pharisee means "separated ones". They were generally ordinary people, not priests, who closely followed Jewish law. Sometimes they extended the ways that these laws were applied to make them even harder to follow. For example, when they said that people must not work on the Sabbath, they meant people could not walk more than about 1km from their house, they could not carry a heavy load or even light a fire in their house.

repentance
If a person repents, it means that they are truly sorry for their sins. Jesus forgave the sins of those people who came to Him and were genuinely sorry for what they had done. But it also means being determined to leave sin behind, trying not to sin at all in future.

resurrection
Three days after Jesus died on the cross, He came back to life, He was resurrected. This is the main and central point of the New Testament, and of Christianity.

Sadducees
These were a group of people smaller than the Pharisees, but more influential. Most of them were members of the family of priests. Most of the information that we have comes from their enemies so is not very reliable. We do know that they did not agree with the extensions of the law that the Pharisees tried to impose on people. This is why the Sadducees did not believe in life after death, as this is not mentioned in the Old Testament.

Samaritan
When the Promised Land was conquered by the Babylonians the Jews were taken away to live in Babylon, a period known as the Exile. The city of Samaria was filled with people from other lands, taken there by the Babylonians. These people were hated by the Jews after this time for taking the Jews' cities. Jesus makes sure that He demonstrates his concern for them, and shows that the kingdom of God is open to everyone by using the Samaritans in his stories.

synagogue
In Jesus's time Jews went to the synagogue to worship, just as they still do today. The synagogue is like the Christian Church. The synagogue also served as the school for local Jewish children.

Index